$TRATEGIES 2000

STRATEGIES 2000

How to Prosper in the New Age

CAROLYN CORBIN

EAKIN PRESS
Austin, Texas

Copyright © 1986
By Carolyn Corbin

Published in the United States of America
By Eakin Press, P.O. Box 23066, Austin, Texas 78735

ALL RIGHTS RESERVED. No part of this book may be reproduced in any form without written permission from the publisher, except for brief passages included in a review appearing in a newspaper or magazine.

ISBN 0-89015-575-5

Library of Congress Cataloging-in-Publication Data

Corbin, Carolyn Pitts, 1946–
　　Strategies 2000.

　　Includes index.
　　1. Finance, Personal—United States. 2. Success. 3. Economic forecasting—United States. 4. United States—Economic conditions—1981–. I. Title.
HG179.C68　1986　332.024　86-14878
ISBN 0-89015-575-5

ESPECIALLY DEDICATED TO
My cousin Gloria Byrd McDonald

Some people influence our lives not so much by what they say as by how they live. Gloria is such a person. She is a successful career woman, exemplary wife and mother, and a consistent blue ribbon prize-winning artist.

Stricken by polio at a young age, her doctors told her she would never walk again—but she did. Through struggle, pain, and continuing to get up many times when it would have been easier to have stayed down, she learned not only to walk but to run, to march as majorette in her high school band, and to dance with the grace of a professional.

Because of her love and genuine concern for people, she chose to change her career in mid-life to nursing. This required re-entry into college, completion of a totally new curriculum, and much hard work. But as is her nature, she achieved her goal.

Soon after beginning her new career, she was confronted with potential blindness. Her doctors gave her one in 10,000 chances of regaining her sight. Through the several months of adjustment that followed, she never lost her enthusiasm for living nor her positive spirit. Against all odds, her sight returned. Again, she overcame.

Throughout her life, with all the joy, pain, adversity, and success, she has kept on trying long after others would have quit.

Her unfaltering faith in God is my example.

Her courage, character, and strength are my inspiration.

Contents

Preface ix
Acknowledgments xi

PART ONE: THE EMERGING NEW CIVILIZATION
   1. The Future is Rushing into the Present   3
   2. The Past is Separating from the Present   7

PART TWO: NEW AGE ECONOMIC TRANSFORMATION
   3. The New Age Economy   19
   4. Seven New Age Economic Conditions   37

PART THREE: STRATEGIES FOR PROSPERITY IN THE 1980s, 1990s, AND BEYOND
   5. Power Positioning   61
   6. Declare Your Independence   67
   7. Anticipate Tomorrow's Business World   95
   8. Develop Resource Connectors   113
   9. Prepare for Predictable Uncertainty   124
   10. Release Yourself to Relate   164
   11. The Beginning   189

Notes   191
Index   202

Preface

Every aspect of our lives is being deeply challenged by new economic and social conditions ushering us deeper into a New Age. In fact, we already live in this New Age — and have been doing so since the early 1970s. We are witnessing unprecedented changes in lifestyle, leisure, labor, and how we achieve success. The rules for well-being of the 1950s, 1960s, and 1970s will often prove counterproductive in future decades. We must apply the new rules if we expect to achieve maximum rewards from career and personal life in the years to come.

At first, you may feel that this is a book on economics. The supporting facts and figures may even bore you somewhat. However, the first four chapters on economics offer important background information for the corporate and personal growth chapters that follow.

The strategies for achievement, prosperity, and self-fulfillment were deduced as a result of economic conditions to which we must respond in the years to come. Economies are a result of how a society conducts its business. Without knowing what is happening, it is difficult to determine what we must do to win the game.

This book is designed to point out to you what is happening to the world in which you live, why we have entered a whole new era with entirely new rules for success, how these massive changes are taking place, and what you can do to achieve a level of well-being unknown to previous generations.

It is my hope that, after completing this work, you will be excited about the opportunities open to you in our new civilization and be inspired to apply these strategies to enhance your peace of mind, maximize your achievement, and increase your faith in tomorrow.

Acknowledgments

Special gratitude to . . .

my husband, Ray, the love of my life.

my mother, Orene Pitts, who taught me not only to talk but to speak.

my father, Ben Pitts, who though no longer alive, inspired hopes, dreams, and aspirations that continue to live within me.

my in-laws, Ray, Coretta, and Linda Corbin, who make my life very special.

Paul E. Koach of IBM, who planted the seeds for this book.

Jean Coupe for her painstaking research, enthusiasm, and loyal friendship.

Sylvia Odenwald for support, encouragement, editing, suggestions, and untold hours spent in compiling information for this work. Without her, this book would never have been written.

PART ONE

The Emerging New Civilization

Chapter 1

The Future Is Rushing Into The Present

Where there is no vision, the people perish.
— Proverbs 29:18

Flight 903's jetliner was approaching the Charlotte, North Carolina airport. The pilot and co-pilot were engaged in general conversation when a signal began beeping loudly. Simultaneously, a red light began to flash. The pilot reached down to disengage the switch but to no avail. The sound continued loudly, and red lights flashed in the darkness of the flight cabin.

Feeling that most certainly there was a short in the electrical system, the flight crew remained rather casual about the warning signals and continued straightway on their flight path while discussing the pros and cons of political issues. The last words on the cockpit recording are "BUT . . . WHERE IS THE AIRPORT?!" The crash was fatal.[1]

The plane had approached the airport too low. The signals were warning the crew that they were too close to the ground. Though the warning signals were there, they were not heeded. The results were literally disastrous.

The Federal Aviation Administration now has seen to it that this particular situation is not likely to occur again by assuring that airlines structure a warning system that cannot be so easily

3

disregarded. But it's too late for the crew and passengers on Flight 903.

Our flashing lights and beepers

Today we too have warning signals — flashing hints of future economic conditions to which we will eventually be called on to respond. If these warnings are ignored, the results could be personal financial fatality. If heeded, these signals could forecast untold prosperity. By properly anticipating and synthesizing these probable conditions, individuals can enter a wave of economic growth unparalleled in United States history.

Based on an eight-year analysis of the nation's major newspapers and financial journals, interviews with financial professionals and economists, an extensive survey of technical literature, and observation of the direction in which our nation is heading, our researchers have defined seven future economic conditions — many of which have already begun to be revealed:

- global and domestic competition
- targeted prosperity
- short shelf-life
- individual responsibility
- convulsive economy
- diversified financial services, and
- premium on human capital.

In Chapter 4, we discuss these conditions in detail.

Note that we are citing economic conditions — not trends. Conditions are composed of trends. According to John Naisbitt in *Megatrends*: "Trends tell you the direction the country is moving in. The decisions are up to you." [2] We can choose, then, whether or not to respond to trends.

Conditions, on the other hand, dictate a state of existence to which we *must* respond. The degree to which we are equipped to make a positive response is determined by

- accuracy in predicting the condition
- preparation for a selected response, and
- resources available to implement a selected strategy.

Historical limits — new rules

The difficulty in anticipating future conditions is that we are limited by historical perspective. Many of the variables that we have used in the past to predict the future no longer work. Society is changing so rapidly that we are being called upon to navigate uncharted waters. The future is rushing into the present at such an alarming pace that we are being forced to apply new rules even before we have learned them well. However, those people who can learn the new rules quickly enough to anticipate future conditions, analyze resources available, and choose a successful response will survive and prosper in the final years approaching the twenty-first century.

Our responses to the new rules of our chameleonic economy will be the single greatest determinant of material success and peace of mind in the next three decades.

Importance of the economy

Most of us think of the economy as being synonymous with money. It involves much more. The economy houses all systems for the production, distribution, and consumption of material wealth. Economies, as we know them, change as a result of social and political power structures, resource supply and demand, availability and quality of production tools and techniques, and cultural values of the people; and this list of economic variables certainly is not exhaustive.

Since World War II, people in the United States have become more interdependent. Very few of us produce and consume our own supplies and necessities as was prevalent before the war. Because of this interdependence, the national economy becomes extremely important to us. Such intangibles as peace of mind, feelings of security, lowered stress level, positive attitude, marital success, and satisfactory lifestyle can be linked directly to the state of the economy. Households have an economy just as a nation does, and this specific economy more directly affects the emotions, feelings, and social systems of a family.

Rapidity of change

Just about everything affects the economy — and change is no exception. In fact, change is occurring so rapidly that most of us must run to keep up with the status quo. Those people who are seventy years of age or older have lived through most of the significant inventions in our total history. Over 85% of the great scientists are living now. These inventions produce changes in how we travel, produce goods and services, communicate, spend leisure time, and literally how we live and die.

As inventions become even more prolific, the rapidity of change will become exponential. As a result, people become confused, burned out, and may even suffer analysis paralysis. Some negative consequences of this rapid change are

- corporate turnover
- corporate productivity slumps
- human indecision (thus draining constructive energy)
- family structural instability
- reduction of self-esteem
- career obsolescence
- financial problems
- emotional stress
- national instability
- spiritual crises, and
- reduction of creativity.

Of course, *all* these factors influence the economy.

However, those people who understand how to deal with change, especially economic change, will hold an edge over those who do not possess the knowledge to challenge these changes when they occur. Financially successful people (and companies) of tomorrow will be those who

- cause and control change
- anticipate change, and
- harness profitable techniques to implement the results of change.

Summary:
1. The economy is a very important determinant of our future well-being.
2. Rapid change is forcing a transition to a New Age Economy.
3. In order to have a financially successful future, we must anticipate future economic conditions to which we must respond.
4. Economic warning signals exist today—survivors will heed them and will prosper.

Chapter 2

The Past Is Separating From The Present

I find the great thing in this world is not so much where we stand as in what direction we are moving.
— Oliver Wendell Holmes

In his book *The Third Wave*, Alvin Toffler describes the period in which we are living as a new civilization with characteristics distinct from all other societies and cultures we have known in the past. This civilization is the third in a series of collective restructurings of our total world; i.e., Toffler terms this new civilization "The Third Wave," which indeed carries with it a new economy, which we will call the "New Age Economy." [1] There were two previous economies, however, that paved the way for our present system. Chart 1 diagrams these three economic waves.

First Wave Economy

The First Wave, according to Toffler, was *distinctly agricultural*. Although we feel tinges of that economy today, its influence is limited. Only a few Americans are now involved in agriculture.

When agriculture reigned as king from several thousand years before the birth of Christ to the mid-1800s here in the United States, productivity from the land was the central issue. In fact, the land dictated the economy. People produced and consumed most of their necessities. If there was a surplus of production over consumption, that quantity was sold or traded for goods, services,

7

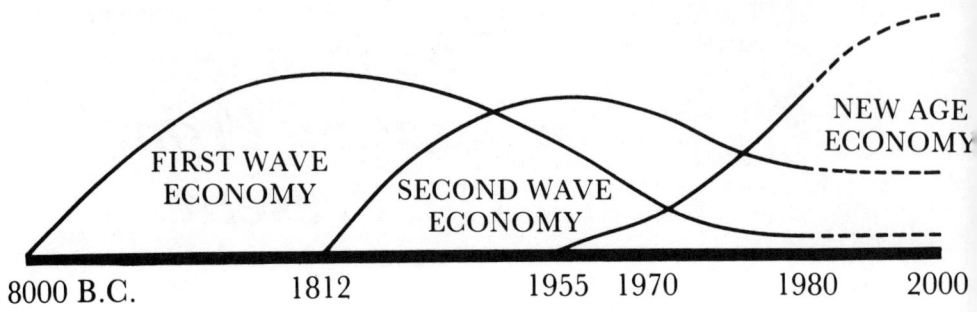

Chart 1
Three Economic Waves

additional animals or seed to enhance next year's production, or even luxury items. The family was the major economic unit.

The people lived relatively isolated in rural areas and built small communities to serve their social, economic, and spiritual needs. Because of their isolation and their ability to produce most necessities, the agricultural people were personally independent but were rarely financially independent (which means being able to live without working and/or depending on money from relatives and other sources). Families were very dependent upon one another for support.

Because of major responsibilities of tending the land and animals, farmers and ranchers were very stationary. Families grew up and rarely wandered from the birth community. It was not unique for several generations to live in a single town. Because of this strong support group, money and saving for the future were not big issues. "Retirement" was not in the vocabulary. People worked until their health no longer permitted them to labor. Health insurance was rare. People paid the doctor or hospital for services rendered by varied means of exchange — and not necessarily money.

The elite of the community were the landowners. Those people who could acquire more and more land became the power figures. Since land was cheap, all one needed was a tough-minded outlook, a penchant for hard work, and an aggressive spirit. Large families were necessary because they provided more people to work the land. Labor was inexpensive or free before 1865 because many slaves were used to multiply yields. Those farmers and ranchers with good agricultural management skills prospered.

Second Wave Economy

When the United States went to war with England in 1812, it had its back against the wall. Before that time, the United States had mostly imported its manufactured goods. England, however, did not look too kindly upon exporting goods to help us survive and win the war. So, as usual, the United States began to get creative and, thereby, to manufacture many of its own products. So began the Second Wave Economy in America (though Toffler cites that the Second Wave began in the 1600s in Europe). Inventors began to design machines that could make people's labors easier. More work could be done in less time. Rather than build such products as cotton gins, reapers, and even rifles by hand, they discovered that most every part could be standardized and mass produced. However, people were needed to assemble the parts, so factories and production lines were created to manufacture these revolutionary items.

Beginning in the Northeast, then, everything about how people lived and worked began to change. Large industries were built around the manufacture of goods and suppliers of these industries. For example, steel and rubber resources were supplied to the manufacturers of farm equipment and, after 1896, the automobile.

Once independent farmers and ranchers moved from their rural life to the city in search of the riches of the industrial age. In the city, these people were no longer able to produce all their food, clothing, and household needs. They were forced to buy these necessities from merchants (or retail outlets) with money they earned from their work. *This new interdependence created another whole new economy—altogether different from the traditional agriculture era.* The United States economy continues to hold great Second Wave influences.

Interdependence among people often leads to abuse and a type of caste system. It was perceived that management abused labor. As a result, members of the Second Wave Economy formed labor unions to unite for what the workers felt were their rights. Though violent at first, the labor negotiations became a big part of the economy—and settled down to peaceful approaches to protest and negotiation. However, the formation of this union movement was to have a very important role in the industrial economy. As the cost of labor became higher, the price of goods was raised to the consumer. After World War II, it was assumed that everyone would receive a raise every year and that the cost of goods and services would escalate also.

With energy cheap and plentiful and capital relatively easy to obtain for expansion, the industrial wave paved the way for the consumptive lifestyle — the good life. Money became the principal means of exchange. People believed that our resources were inexhaustible and that each year brought more prosperity. *The elite of this wave were the great business tycoons and politicians.* Success was considered quantitative and measured by material possessions and money. Those who acquired vast empires had to be competitive, aggressive, and had to have good business management skills. *The major economic units were the corporation and an ever-enlarging government.*

From 1812 to the mid-1960s, America grew into an industrial empire — the likes of which the world had never known. To handle the complexities of a mobile, urban society with the population growing by leaps and bounds, a new economic system was implemented. Order was produced from chaos. Statistics were gathered and analyzed, and the economy became relatively predictable.

CREATION OF THE FEDERAL RESERVE SYSTEM

Business bankruptcies along with general economic downturns during this period caused periodic financial panics. This led to failures of a large number of banks. To stabilize both the banking and monetary systems, the Federal Reserve System was established by the Federal Reserve Act of 1913. Though this central bank is independent, it must report to Congress. The basic goals are to supervise U. S. currency and influence credit. It adapts its policies to periods of inflation, disinflation, and depression as the economy dictates.

The Federal Reserve System has a board of governors who

- set member bank reserve requirements
- approve discount rates at which banks can borrow money
- manage protection rules for consumers of financial institutions, and
- supervise the twelve Federal Reserve Banks.

The Past is Separating From the Present

The twelve Federal Reserve Banks
- propose discount rates at which member banks may borrow money
- keep reserves for member banks
- lend to member banks at the discount window
- distribute coin and currency
- collect checks
- clear checks
- distribute funds
- examine banks, and
- operate the mechanism of government debt and balances of cash.

With the ability to influence changes in monetary policy, the chairman of the board of governors is one of the most powerful people in the United States. The chairman is appointed by the president of the United States, as are the other six board members.

At the end of 1983, approximately 38% of all U. S. commercial banks belonged to the Federal Reserve System. Since the original act of 1913, there have been several amendments. Included are the Banking Act of 1935, Bank Holding Company Act amendments of 1970, International Banking Act of 1978, Full Employment and Balanced Growth Act of 1978, and Depository Institutions Deregulation and Monetary Control Act of 1980.[2]

Economic complexities which developed in the industrial era, then, led to eventual need for more control and regulation of monetary and credit policy. Thus, standardization and synchronization became trademarks not only of industrial production but also of the economy.

PREDICTABLE ECONOMIC CYCLES

One theory of economic prediction was developed during the industrial era by the Russian economist Nikolai D. Kondratieff. His principal work on his long-wave economic cycles — the Kondratieff Wave — was published in 1925.[3] For several years, the theory seemed to predict crests and troughs in the economy. However, it lacked a true model. Since that time such economists as Jay Forrester of Massachusetts Institute of Technology have developed models based on empirical data of the U.S. economy that closely correlate with Kondratieff's theory.

According to Kondratieff, the capitalist economies of the Western world had undergone two and one-half cycles from 1800 to 1925.[4] He accurately predicted the Great Depression of the 1930s by using such economic measures as commodity production, consumption, prices, and interest rates for forecasting.

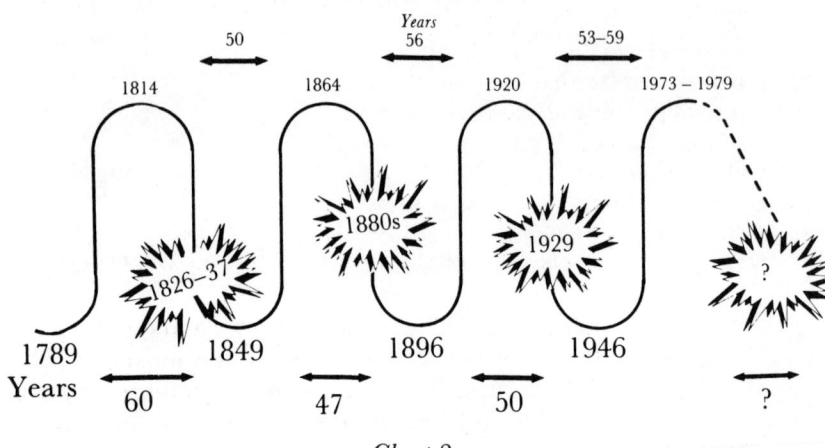

Chart 2
Economic Cycles

This combination model of Kondratieff and Forrester is shown in Chart 2. Causes of these cycles are yet to be determined, but Kondratieff indicates that they are self-correcting.

Note that there are fifty to sixty years between the boom times, i.e., the crests; and there are forty-seven to sixty years between the troughs, or the bottoming-out periods after a crash. The explosive areas are the actual crash periods in the economy, which occur historically every nine to twenty-four years from the peak periods.[5]

The industrial economy was largely driven by finite energy sources and theoretically would follow the Kondratieff Wave. If predictable, the fourth wave should have crested in the early 1970s with an economic crash coming between 1979 and 1994.[6] Between the years 1996 and 2010, we should bottom out and begin to recover. *For those industries tied to the industrially dominated Second Wave, only time will tell whether this wave theory continues to predict the economy.* Those industries tied to this era—automobile, steel, rubber, oil, trucking, and airlines to name a few—did suffer heavily in the early 1980s. Some people even considered some of these industries to be in depression, though that economic downturn was very narrowly defined.

INSTITUTIONAL DEPENDENCY

The rise of corporate dominance created a dependence on the corporation not only for financial well-being, but also for substitute activities normally provided by the family and community during the agricultural wave.

Employee benefits were created for labor — mainly because of union pressures. Corporations began to provide pensions, health care, vacation, sick leave, bonuses, rest periods, profit-sharing, and other programs. Total benefit payments, according to *Employee Benefits Historical Data* published by the U. S. Chamber of Commerce, grew from $1.5 billion in 1929 to in excess of $400 billion today.[7] It became a possibility to eventually live without working, i.e., to retire. This option was heretofore only available to society's elite — not the average worker. These added benefits created financial help but fueled a false security — especially to those veterans of the World War II era.

After the Great Depression, people began to look to bigger government for protection and security. More taxation of the people and expanded spending by the government was needed to support such a large, people-dependent system. A whole new discipline in the financial industry was created as a result: tax preparation, analysis, and sheltering techniques. Laws became more complicated, demanding that accounting and legal professionals set up practices that aided individuals and corporations in interpretation and application of the tax code.

Social Security and Medicare payments eventually rose to become slightly over 27% of the U.S. budget. For many family units, this government benefit provides almost 40% of income and the sole health care plan.

Toward the end of the Second Wave, 1973–1982, the big institutions began to fail the people. Promises could not always be kept. Many people, especially those in or nearing retirement, could not fulfill their future dreams.

DEMOGRAPHIC EXPLOSION

Population makeup and sheer numbers have always affected the economy. After World War II, between 1946 and 1961, the number of babies born was phenomenal — thus being called the baby boom generation. Their education level, career aspirations, labor and housing needs, lifestyle, and income level are greatly impacting that economy that we knew in the industrial era. Their need for jobs and their ability to adjust to change is challenging workers in the mid-fifties age group. Industries directly connected with the Second Wave Economy are offering "sweetened" retirement programs—not only to cut costs but also to make room for the young, aggressive labor force. People who planned to retire from companies at an older age are finding that early retirement can be enticing and are opting to take advantage of the opportunity.

The industrial era has created a group of retirees and future retirees who will make heavy demands on both corporate and government pension programs. The drains on these systems have yet to be realized. The solutions have yet to be formulated.

CONSUMPTIVE LIFESTYLE

Every year gets better. Lifestyle can be leveraged in order to "have now" and "pay later." These are two of the economic philosophies fostered in the Second Wave. Because of surplus production, promises of large institutions, and many good years after World War II, U. S. society became very consuming—rather than saving and investing. Even tax laws support deductions for spending rather than saving. The invention of the credit card in the mid-1950s challenged the self-discipline of many Americans, who on the average save only 3% to 8% of income anyway.

According to a 1984 *Money* magazine survey entitled "Americans and Their Money":

- 70% of Americans have outstanding loans
- 81% hold credit cards
- 43% would have trouble paying an unexpected bill for $1,000
- 49% have less than $5,000 in savings.[8]

Producing a generation concerned with self-fulfillment, Second Wave Americans' dreams became closely allied with the economy. If it expanded, so did their options. When it collapsed into recession, so did their lifestyle. The consumptive philosophy was in full bloom by 1969. *People believed that resources were infinite and that a child's future was always better than that of his parents.*[9]

WHEN WAVES COLLIDE

The First and Second Wave economies are largely workable systems of the past. Now a new civilization is dawning, and people are confused by the collision of economies. Bits and pieces of

The Past is Separating From the Present

agriculture still exist along with heavy industrial influence. Yet still another system is being inaugurated. Many are trying to restabilize these mature systems of the past in order to seek comfort and to retreat to a known world — a world into which they were born and in which their families lived and died. *However, those worlds of the past, once perceived as safe, are becoming perilous.* Security lies in separating from them and in looking to the future. Prosperous individuals will have the ability to meet the challenges of the New Age Economy.

Summary:

1. The United States is inaugurating a new civilization which brings a New Age Economy — the third in a series of collective restructurings of one total economic system.
2. For thousands of years until 1812, the First Wave Economy was mainly driven by agriculture with the family being the basic economic unit.
3. The Second Wave Economy, reaching significance in the United States in 1812, emphasized industrialism and big government. The corporation and U.S. government were the basic economic units.
4. In 1913, the Federal Reserve System was established to supervise U.S. currency and to influence credit. The Federal Reserve has seven governors, twelve Federal Reserve Banks, and many commercial member banks.
5. When compared with empirical data, the Kondratieff Wave theory, formulated in 1925 by Russian Nikolai D. Kondratieff, has been able to predict three major economic peaks, valleys, wars or conflicts, and economic crashes in U.S. history since 1800. The big question is . . . "Is its 'predict-ability' still workable in the New Age Economy?"
6. Especially after World War II, the American people became dependent upon corporations and the government for economic security.
7. Baby boom demographics are changing the entire economic emphasis from the way we work to the way we spend time and money.
8. An era of plenty and optimism after World War II fostered the consumption ethic in America. "Buy now, pay later" became the philosophy with the 1950s inception of the credit card.
9. Three economies are now colliding: two fleeing into the past; one carrying us into the future. Generally, people are confused and question which system will bring security and prosperity.

PART TWO

New Age Economic Transformation

Chapter 3

The New Age Economy

The lowest ebb is the turn of the tide.
— Henry Wadsworth Longfellow

The world appears to be turning upside down. People in every walk of life are confused about the future. The present produces an uneasy sense of well-being while, at the same time, news reports of world events, trade deficits, and budget questions loom large in the minds of the American people. We are beginning to view the future with cautious, uneasy optimism — as if there could be some doubt as to the direction our economy could ultimately take. What Americans are experiencing are the birth pangs of the New Age Economy.

These insecure feelings are normal during any transition period. Just as an infant is hurled with great shock from its mother's womb into a new world, we are speeding from our safe environment into a new economy with equal anxiety, shock, and questioned expectations. Some people are asking: "How do we know we have entered into a new era? Couldn't we simply be headed toward another economic downturn or, worse, to total destruction?"

Evidence supports the fact that we are on two courses simultaneously — as eras collide. Industries adhering to the Second Wave philosophy might be on a crash course, while those industries clinging to a New Age philosophy, for the most part, will be able to survive the transition to the next economy.

Economic factors cause economic conditions

Just as the interaction of atmospheric variables produces different combinations of weather conditions, so various economic factors can interact to produce varied economic conditions. Each time we have changed from one economic wave to another, there have been five simultaneous social shifts that have taken place. The result of these shifts has been redefinition and reweighting of economic variables. It happened going from First to Second Wave, and it is happening again in the transition from Second Wave to New Age economic dominance. The five simultaneous social changes to watch for are

- power shifts
- significant demographic changes
- unusual rapidity of technological innovation
- changes in dominant social institutions, and
- changes in industrial emphasis.

The basic economic variables operational in the First Wave were *energy* and *people*. As we show in Diagram 1, the major sources of energy to drive the agricultural economy were domesticated animals and humans themselves. Since these sources could be created on the farms through reproductive methods, they were relatively inexpensive and were readily available in ample supply. Though one unit of energy source was finite (through physical death, injury or aging) that unit could be replaced by a similar unit.

The labor supply was normally from family members, slave labor before 1865, inexpensively hired help, and/or through bartering arrangements. However, when these five simultaneous social changes evolved, energy and labor were redefined and a third variable, *capital*, was added.[1] Thus, we entered the Second Wave Economy after 1812 when:

- *Power* shifted from the farm to the city, from the farmer to big government and big business, and from the family to the corporation.
- *Demographic changes* occurred. Populations dominated cities as opposed to rural communities. Groups of people (i.e., unions, mass market, etc.) had even more power and respect

The New Age Economy

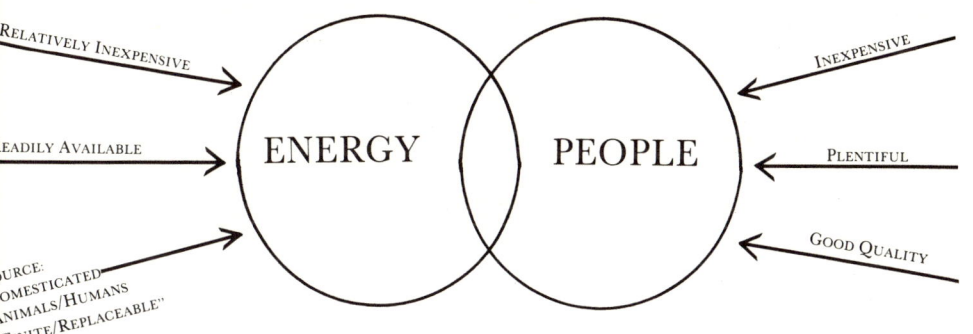

Diagram 1
First Wave Economy

than individual family economic units. People began to live longer, age, and to become more mobile.
- Beginning in 1812, *new inventions* to help farmers do their work more productively and to mass produce textiles and other needed supplies began to appear rapidly due to America's being at war with its major supplier, England. Inventions produced rapid change, new job opportunities, and made many farmers, even though they remained on the farm, Second Wave businessmen.
- No longer was the family the dominant institution, but government shared rank with corporations for *institutional dominance*. The elite of the communities switched from large landowners to politicians and corporate tycoons.
- Major *emphasis* shifted from agriculture as a major industry to manufacturing of heavy equipment, railroads, cars, and airplanes, and production of steel, oil, rubber, glass, and various alloy metals.
- As industrial emphasis changed, the primary energy source switched from animals/humans to petroleum and its byproducts.

With these transitional shifts in place, the basic economic variables became not only the interaction of people and energy but also a third variable, *capital*. When these three factors were inexpensive and plentiful, the economy was generally very produc-

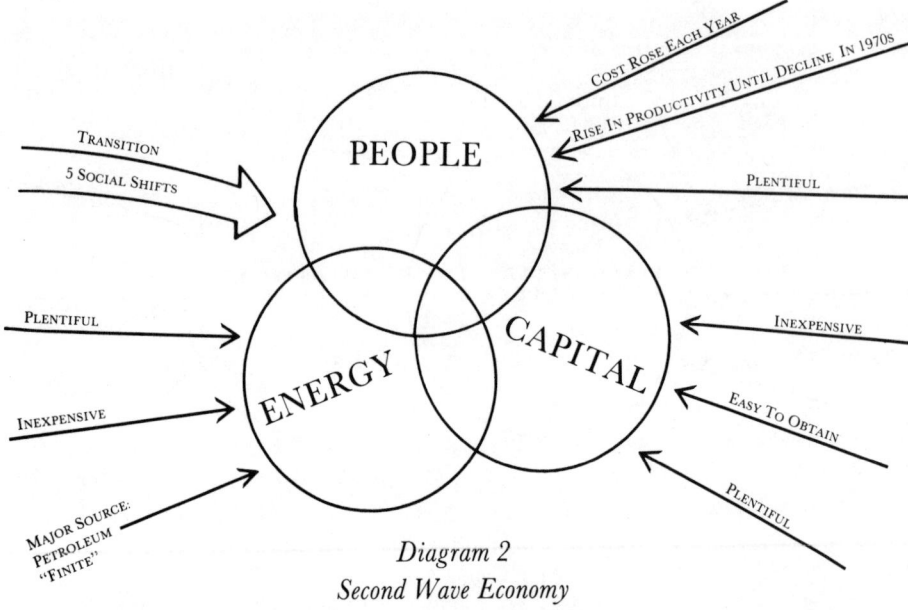

Diagram 2
Second Wave Economy

tive. In fact, if capital and energy were relatively inexpensive to obtain even though the cost of labor continued to rise, the wheels of industry could continue to turn, and the economy would do well.

In the isolationist, industrial economy of the Second Wave (see Diagram 2), *energy* was relatively plentiful and inexpensive, *money* for expansion was easy to obtain, interest rates for borrowing were acceptable, and *labor* costs were assumed to rise every year. These additional expenses were passed on to the consumer in the form of rising prices—and the consumer largely accepted this situation as normal as long as productivity was also rising. To expand, industry merely had to call on the consumer to help.

Second Wave economic conditions

The resultant economic conditions from interactions of these variables to which our parents, grandparents, and, to a great extent, we have been called on to respond are:

- Economically predictable business cycles (see the Kondratieff Wave Theory in Chapter 2)
- Mass prosperity, recession or depression (i.e., the nation as a whole suffers or prospers)
- Predictable dependence on the government and big corporations

The New Age Economy

- U. S. economic supremacy in the world
- Increased generational prosperity — children automatically have better economic conditions than their parents
- Products and people with a long period of usefulness in the marketplace
- Measurable performance criteria as opposed to quality and creativity as the benchmarks of success

Obviously, people's strategies for surviving and prospering under these conditions have proven effective, for we have just passed through the most affluent times in American history.

Like changing atmospheric factors, however, there is evidence that the weighting and redefinition of economic variables is again rapidly shifting and will introduce still new economic conditions to which we must respond. It is the varying of these factors that helps to explain what is ushering in our New Age Economy. It is

- the source, cost, and availability of *natural resources*
- types and costs of such a *medium of exchange* as money to finance production and expansion
- availability, productivity, attitude and cost of *people* for labor, and
- the degree of *competition* in the marketplace during a specific *time frame* that gives new meaning to our economic conditions. Note that competition is an added variable beyond the Second Wave Economy.

These four factors have tremendous impact on how companies will be managed and on how products and services will be marketed and sold in the future.

Five basic social shifts again have taken place over the last decade and are continuing to mature into the twenty-first century. They have again reweighted and redefined the Second Wave economic variables. The shifts are

- shared domestic and international power
- unprecedented technological innovation and change
- demographic restructuring — especially age groupings
- altered institutional dominance to individual, self-power, and
- revised industrial emphasis on process rather than product.

THE FIVE SOCIAL SHIFTS NOW TAKING PLACE

Shared power

The United States has the largest national economy in the world. However, its isolationist supremacy is being seriously challenged today by other countries. The major areas of growth are in the Far East in such countries as Japan, South Korea, Taiwan, Hong Kong, and Singapore.[2] These areas, however, are experiencing their real growth in Second Wave manufacturing-type industries. The United States can continue its lead by moving to an emphasis in New Age information-type industries. The power for these types of industries will likely be shared by the European arena as well as the Soviet Union. China is appearing to be a great contender for sharing economic supremacy within the next twenty years.

As more and more countries become economically powerful, they become serious competitors to the economic supremacy America has claimed since the mid-1800s. With more countries competing with the United States, not only for product development but also for quality of products and services offered, the American consumer has more choices. Not only do we have American products in our marketplace, but also products that are imported from other countries. This situation provides a real advantage to the American consumer. However, it causes competition among American industries and decreases the profits that many industries knew in the past. Each member of such Second Wave-type industries as steel, mining, oil and gas, shipbuilding, machine tools, airlines, or other oil- and gas-driven industries, are getting a smaller piece of the economic pie than they did a decade ago. Many businesses are forced to be more creative in their operations, and still many other businesses are by default going bankrupt.

Unprecedented technological innovation

If we could take the last 50,000 years and condense them into a fifty-year period, here is how the breakdown of time would have taken place:

Period of Time	*Event*
50 years ago	Neanderthal man in prime
10 years ago	People stopped living in caves
5 years ago	Communication was via written pictures
6 months ago	Printing press was invented
1 month ago	Electric lamp invented
3 weeks ago	Wright brothers flew
1.5 weeks ago	First jet flew

The New Age Economy

1 week ago	First television sold to the public
yesterday	First American astronaut was in space
seconds ago	Man landed on the moon
nanoseconds ago	U.S. celebrated 200 years of freedom[3]

The speed with which technological innovations are taking place is unprecedented in the United States. "Surveys project a ten-fold growth in the next decade both in numbers of personal computers and in central processing capacity." This was a statement made by John Diebold in his article entitled "New Challenges for the Information Age" (*Futurist,* June 1985).[4] Rapid innovation rushing out of a period of calm stability has profound effect on the American people. Vast changes made so quickly not only invigorate the economy but also cause vast individual and social changes. The ability to sort out valuable information and capitalize on the information industry will foster economic well-being in the United States. Historically, rapid innovation has carried the United States out of a depressed period into economic prosperity and has developed many ancillary industries to service its primary innovations. The New Age Economy is characterized by such information industries as robotics, fiber optics, lasers, electronics, telecommunications equipment, artificial intelligence, and biotechnology. It is the servicing, employment, and byproducts of these industries that will fuel the fires of economic freedom in the decades to come.

During periods of rapid innovation, however, the American people have found it difficult to cope with change. High stress levels occur, new education must take place, and many people find themselves without jobs because they refuse to retrain for the new industries which are replacing many of the old, once-considered-stable industries.

Growth and change are accelerating at exponential rates. For example:

- In 1850, there were four cities with a population of greater than one million. In 1900, there were nineteen cities with a population of greater than one million. Today there are in excess of 140 cities with a population greater than one million.
- One-half of the energy consumed in the past 2,000 years has been used in the last 200 years.
- One-half of all products on supermarket shelves were not there a decade ago and will likely not be there a decade from now.

- For a child who is ten years old today, there will be four times as much knowledge available to that child when he goes to college as is available to him now. When that ten-year-old child becomes fifty years of age, knowledge will have increased by thirty-two times today's level.

People who are seventy years of age or older today have seen most of the technological innovation that has taken place in the United States. It is almost staggering to the mind to believe that most of the people living today have actually seen and experienced a total technological revolution in America.

Technological change, then, will be a tremendous contributor to New Age economic prosperity.

Shifting demographic structure

To paraphrase the late U. S. President John F. Kennedy: "The torch has [again] been passed to a new generation of Americans." Based on data from the U. S. Bureau of the Census, we find that approximately one-third of our population are considered products of the baby boom era. These people range in age today from approximately twenty-four years of age to forty years of age. Throughout their transition over time, they have tremendously affected the American economy. Schools, jobs, the military, baby food, clothing, housing and automobile markets, and other consumer goods have all felt the impact of the baby boom generation. Along with this huge demographic thrust came a new philosophy that impacted self-fulfillment, career, world markets, and even an attitude toward time and change. This same population will be aging during the next thirty years. Tremendous impact will be felt on our Social Security system as these people begin to retire in the year 2010. By that time there will probably be two workers supporting each one worker who is retired. Social Security restructuring may take place in order to support these people who will: (a) exist in tremendous numbers and (b) draw from the system longer.

The major demographic shift that is taking place is from a youth-oriented culture to an aging culture. This will have profound effect on the labor force, product marketing, the leisure industry, health care, housing and supporting product lines, and government benefit systems. At this time, just under 12% of the population is over sixty-five years of age. Of those people born between 1930 and 1936 during the Great Depression, there will be fewer in number because the birth rate steadily declined and did not begin to increase until after 1936 when the United States felt that it was coming out of the depressed years into prosperity. By the year 2000, persons sixty-five and older are expected to represent 13% of our population; and by the year 2030, people sixty-five years or older will represent in excess of 20% of the population according to a 1984 report from the American Association of Retired Persons entitled "A Profile of Older Americans." [5]

Demographic restructuring also affects the philosophy of the New Age Economy. The baby boom generation generally shares a "buy now, pay later" attitude. Those people born toward the end of the baby boom era share a more conservative philosophy than those people born from 1946 to 1955. The reason for this shift from extreme consumption to conservative consumption is the energy crisis which occurred first in 1973–74 and repeated itself in 1978–79. People who were born toward the end of the baby boom remember that deprivation and the feeling that comes from realizing that our energy sources are finite. These people were impacted at an impressionable time in their lives in such a way that they will probably carry a more conservative attitude into the twenty-first century. They will buy for quality and durability, as opposed to buying on impulse and throwing items away if they don't last or meet their specific purposes.

People born during the early years of the baby boom generation are more wasteful and perhaps even more optimistic than people born during the latter years. This situation will affect business in that the people from ages thirty-five to forty will be concentrated in the management of our major industries after the year 1990. In fact, very soon more than half of management will be over forty years of age — more than likely causing a general optimism and expansion in business. There will be much fallout from businesses who have overexpanded, miscalculated, and mismanaged due to optimism that was unfounded.

Working as subordinates to these people will be the more conservative, less economically fortunate baby boomers who are in their mid to late twenties. These people suffered high interest rates in getting into their first home — even if they could afford their first home. They suffered recessions trying to get into the job market, and many of them did not get jobs in the career areas that they worked so hard for in college. Many of these people today are highly educated but, due to the crisis in the oil industry and related products of the Second Wave, many of these people are not meeting their career goals and are becoming frustrated.

As this one-third of the population grows older, there will be additional frustrations and additional limits on finance and income — especially if these people continue to try to find employment and to train themselves in Second Wave industries rather than moving to New Age information and service industries.

The philosophy of self-fulfillment fostered by the baby boomers of college age in the 1960s will find itself evidenced especially in marketing. No longer in the New Age Economy will there be mass markets, but there will be "niched" markets. Markets will be not only for products and services of corporations, but we can also expand the term to be internal markets in corporations. We will see business operations that are employee-driven rather than management-driven, and we will see the market thrust of corporations being buyer-driven and not seller-driven as we have known in the past. Because of a need for self-fulfillment, a need to be heard, and a desire for personal choice, business and industry will be run totally differently by the turn of the century than it is run today. Everything from market analysis and application to employee benefits will be restructured to fit individual needs and niched markets.

Another implication of the demographic shift is that people will be more inclined to convenience and time-saving opportunities. Supermarkets will be really "super" in that they will have all sorts of shopping opportunities available. Under one roof will be housed everything from travel agencies to automated teller machines to pharmacies to gourmet cooking items. Evidence is showing that even automobile dealers are merging to put all their dealerships under one gigantic roof so that people can shop for automobiles much as they would shop in a mall for comparative pricing and shopping.

Convenience items will be best sellers. People will be willing to pay more to save time. This advent is the result not only of a consumptive attitude, but it is also the result of the fact that there are more two-career couples than ever before. Because of the time constraints on domestic chores and cooking, there will be more emphasis on healthful fast foods, robotics to do mundane domestic chores, and other services for the household. These types of industries will grow prolifically until about 2005 to 2010, when these people then begin to shift toward retirement housing. At that point, unless there is an influx of population through immigration (even if these people could afford the type of housing that is now available), then there should be a buyer's market for houses.

Beginning in the year 2010, many of the single-family homes will be too large for retired people and will be put on the market. Services for the household will be shifting to services for retired people. Looking at the states that are heavily concentrated for older people, we find that Florida has most of the over-sixty-five population (17% of total population), followed by Arkansas, Rhode Island, Iowa, Pennsylvania, South Dakota, and Missouri (14% each). By observing these populations and the goods and services that are supportive of these populations, we will find the generally productive industries by the year 2010. Of course, these industries will evolve, and they will not be the same as they are now. But the general industry categories will be significant for people to look into for investments as well as for future career opportunities.

Altered institutional dominance

There has been a shift in cultural dominance of major institutions from the past to the present. During the First Wave, the major institution was the family. During the Second Wave, the major institutions were the corporation and the government. And in the New Age Economy, the major institution will be the individual. The major emphasis in the New Age Economy will be on individual, or self-fulfillment. Many people view this as a negative philosophy. However, it probably is one of the best things that has ever happened to America. In the turmoil resulting from the search for self-fulfillment out of the 1960s and 1970s, we have a resulting shift in the definition of what people want out of life as well as a basic definition of success.

In a survey which I conducted with over 200 subjects throughout 1984, a spiritual definition of success was consistently ranked higher than a *material* definition of success. In other words, when the respondents were asked what they felt success would be, most of them listed "peace of mind, good friends, a happy family, and a career they enjoyed." When asked to rank order twelve items, these four items consistently ranked at the top. Consistently ranking at the bottom were material items such as a big house and an expensive automobile. These 200 people were representative of a cross section of America from ages twenty-three through sixty. So, even though people are searching for self-fulfillment, this can be translated into a more intangible quest for success and well-being.

People are gaining more self-confidence in that they do not feel that their success depends upon what other people think of them. Rather than being so other-directed, these people are becoming more inner-directed. They are beginning to know that in order to help the world, they have to help themselves. The trend in the New Age Economy will be to help the individual, not only in work but also to help the individual relate to other people better. With people having much of the manual labor done for them, and even many of their mental efforts replaced by computers, for the first time in American history, in fact in world history, we will be *released to relate. This will be one of the most profound effects of the New Age Economy.*

Dr. Jonas Salk, who won renowned acclaim in 1954 for the development of the first polio vaccine, has spent the last decade researching and writing about the future of humankind. He feels that the metabiological equivalent of the biological gene is an idea generated in the human mind. The last frontier in America that we have to conquer is the human mind. At this point, we know less about that entity than we do about almost anything else in the world. Dr. Salk believes that the development of human relationships — of sharing information and of good communication — will be essential to the survival of the human species in the universe. Ideas and creativity, he cites, are no longer luxuries; they will be necessities in the future.[6] Wisdom will be as essential as physical fitness for the well-being of humankind. As we mature mentally, as we already have physically, it will be essential that humans learn to relate in a peaceful manner or else we will destroy ourselves. The media indicates that humankind is equipped at this very moment to destroy itself in a period of eighteen minutes.[7]

The New Age Economy is so exciting because for the first time in human history we have gotten away from the quest for materialism and arrived at a need for spiritualism — for that intangible peace of mind that comes when we develop stable relationships not only among ourselves as citizens of our great country, but also among all nations so that we can peacefully coexist.

Revised industrial emphasis

In the Second Wave Economy, major industries concentrated on their products or results. In the New Age Economy, the primary industrial focus will be on process, i.e., on the information that generates the product or result. In other words, there is a shift from *what* to *how* in the new era. Second Wave industries traditionally produced such items as automobiles without emphasis on fuel economy or pollution control. The airline industry produced airplanes without tremendous consideration of the need for reduction in fuel consumption, fire-retardant materials, or some safety standards that are now being implemented.

Today and into the future there will be more and more concentration on how these same products and services can be information-driven. Realizing that our Second Wave energy source, petroleum, is finite and not self-replacing, there will be emphasis on such New Age energy sources as the sun and other alternatives. Heretofore, rarely was it questioned that each year employees would get a raise whether or not their productivity had increased a great deal over the previous year's performance. In the New Age, there will be a concentration on the process of getting the product and service to the marketplace with the best quality and excellence and best consistency. This will breed the replacement of a lot of people who do mundane repetitive chores with robots who can work at a steady level, not take lunch breaks, and not stop to have conversation from time to time. This whole industrial process will breed a new elite in our society. Whereas during the First Wave the elite were the landowners, and the Second Wave elite were business and government officials, the New Age elite will be *proprietors of information*. Those who *know how* to produce products and services with quality and excellence and those people who *know how* to get repeat business from customers as well as to streamline industries for greatest profitability will be the most respected in the New Age. These individuals will command high income and tremendous benefits from corporations as well as from society. People who possess appropriate information will possess the keys to national defense, to economic prosperity, and, perhaps, even to world peace.

Because of all the information on processes that will eventually be available by the twenty-first century and because this information will be so public, there will be a tremendous need for *sharing* rather than for *competition*. During the first agricultural wave, citizens were largely self-producing. Moving into the Second Wave — emphasizing industry and big government — people became very interdependent, yet there was still much drive to compete. Although a general interdependence was created among people for products and services, there was still secrecy and privacy of information in order to obtain a competitive edge. Not only did this occur within the United States, but the United States is also doing it as a ploy for defense against other nations. These nations, in turn, are using privacy and proprietary information as a defense against the United States. Therefore, powers rise against others through competition.

During the New Age Economy, and during a time when information will be so easy to obtain, it seems that the only answer will be sharing of information. If everybody has access to the same information, then competitiveness will give rise to sharing. No longer will there be a we-they attitude among employees and management; a team approach will ensue because of the need to share information and work in order to get the job accomplished.

Process-oriented industries will lead to more choices among where we live and work. We moved from a totally isolated agricultural economy to an urban industrial economy, and in the New Age people will be able to scatter themselves across the United States yet continue to work for a company of their choice. Great distances can be traveled through speedy mass transit and through communications equipment. People will not necessarily have to be physically located at the corporate site but can be connected to the corporation through communication devices and satellite systems. More choices of housing and locations will decrease the need for mobility as a lifestyle. Not only has the information economy bred a decrease in mobility for corporations, but also the fact that more and more couples have dual careers (as well as the need to watch the bottom line) has caused corporations to decrease the number of moves that their employees make per year. IBM has reported that because of two-income couples and more advanced communications techniques, only 3% of its work force relocates annually. This is a significant decrease from times past when the acronym "IBM" among its employees sometimes meant, "I've Been Moved." Such historically mobile companies as IBM are helping their people find career growth opportunities where they are. In many corporations, it is no problem if a person refuses to relocate.

Thus, the industrial focus on process as opposed to product will change the entire framework of industrial operations. These five significant social changes work together to redefine the basic economic variables—and when these factors are reorganized and redefined, it initially becomes difficult to predict the economic future until data can be gathered and applied. This is the situation in which the United States finds itself today—in the transition between economic waves with no solid data for prediction and extrapolation.

NEW AGE ECONOMIC VARIABLES

The resulting redefinition of variables of the New Age Economy follow:

- the degree of *competition* in the marketplace;
- availability, productivity, attitude, and cost of *people* for labor;
- the source, cost, and availability of *natural resources;*
- types and costs of such a *medium of exchange* as money to finance production and expansion.

Competition

Shared power among nations, individuals, and corporations has led to competition being included as a major variable affecting the New Age Economy.

Increasing competition both on a domestic and world basis has changed pricing and profit structure immensely. No longer can prices simply be raised and passed to the consumer when the competitors may have found ways to maximize the values of the other three critical economic variables and can give the consumer a better product for an equal or lesser price.

People

Shifting demographics, especially the large, aggressive baby boom generation, has changed both the productivity and philosophy of the labor force. Even sheer numbers competitively vying for similar positions is changing the character of the labor force. By 1990, the baby boomers will account for 54% of all workers.[8] Being accustomed to making demands and creating changes, baby boomers will want to stress experiential process of work equal to the material rewards of the career. Loyalty to corporations will continue to decrease because baby boomers have always been self-dependent and oriented to self-fulfillment. Turnover in the labor force will continue to proliferate. Total devotion to job will decline as they pursue interests outside the corporation.[9]

Along with demographic changes, altered institutional dominance is changing the labor force. Dominance is shifting from the corporate/political arena to emphasis on the worth of the individual. This combination of factors is restructuring the labor variable. In the latter years of the Second Wave, labor was high in cost, declining in quality, and high in availability. In the New Age, labor will increase in quality due to replacement of people with robots. The human labor force will be priced according to performance (i.e., commissions, self-employment, profit-sharing, bonus plans, and independent contractors) and will be highly educated and plentiful in availability, although not necessarily in applicability to positions open, until about 2030. There will be great opportunity for portions of the work force but also much unemployment among those who fail to adapt to changing labor needs.

Natural Resources

When primarily using finite energy sources over which a nation does not have total control, there is always the possibility of demand exceeding supply, thereby increasing cost significantly. Additionally, there is probability of embargoes and price fluctuation vacillating with world conditions. A great percentage of the world's tin, rubber, and oil supplies could be strategically blocked by severe U. S. troubles with Asia and/or the Middle East. Materials important to the Pentagon—platinum, manganese, chromium, vanadium, cobalt—could be cut off if there is conflict between the U. S. and South Africa.[10]

As the energy source becomes more difficult to obtain, it becomes more costly to find and process. This situation exists today with oil as America's major energy source. As this is written, there is a temporary oil glut. However, the two past energy crises emphasized the U. S.'s lack of total control over its supplies as well as the finiteness of this natural resource.

The New Age Economy will explore energy source alternatives. Although expensive at first, they will eventually be perfected and will drive energy costs down. Shell Oil Company, Texaco, Inc., and Southern California Edison are now experimenting with coal gasification as an alternative to nuclear power, which is more expensive and more politically abrasive.[11] There seems to be a 200-year supply of coal in the U. S. alone.

Renewable solar energy will also be explored. Some utilities and private firms will continue to test nuclear plants but will be closely regulated by the federal government.

Objectives in the New Age Economy include:
- secure more control of natural resources
- gradually reduce cost of use, and
- define a renewable resource to drive industry.

Means of exchange

Availability of capital to be exchanged for business growth and expansion competes with capital needed to repay government debt and decreased purchasing power due to inflation—just to name a couple of influences on the supply, cost, and demand for finite capital.

In the New Age Economy, traditional capital, which is surplus of production over consumption, will be scarce and costly. Due to heavy international debt, deregulation of the financial services industry, and the huge domestic budget deficit coupled with tremendous trade deficits, businesses and government will be forced to be more creative in securing a means of exchange for future growth. This is the reason why we are labeling this variable in the broader sense rather than limiting it to traditional capital of the Second Wave Economy. The restructuring of this variable alone has great influence on new economic conditions and will be discussed in detail in Chapter 4.

Yes! We have entered a New Age Economy.

Distinctive differences exist in the new economic climate into which we are rapidly catapulting—much of which is already in place. The vast differences among the three economic waves are listed in the chart that follows.

Those people who participate in this New Age with wisdom, finesse, and vigor will reap untold, exciting rewards.

	Agricultural	*Industrial*	*New Age*
Production/Consumption Dependency:	Independent	Interdependent	Intradependent
Living Style:	Isolated	Urban	Interglobal
Basic Economic Unit:	Family	Corporation/Government	Self
Cultural Space Orientation:	Stationary	Mobile	Technologically Interconnected
Society's Elite:	Landowners	Business Tycoons/Politicians	Proprietors of Information
Personal Success Philosophy:	Physical Strength	Material Well-Being	Spiritual Balance

Chart 3
Economic Wave Differences

Summary:
1. People are puzzled about the direction in which our economy is moving.
2. During each wave, economic factors have combined in a definite way to cause economic conditions.
3. When five specific social changes simultaneously occur over a fifty- to sixty-year period, that signals immersion into a transition period to a new economy.
4. During the past fifty years, these five significant social changes have occurred — redefining and shifting economic variables. Therefore, we can surmise that the New Age Economy is evolving.
5. Distinctive differences exist in the New Age Economy — causing it to stand unique among the three total economies since 8000 B.C.

Chapter 4

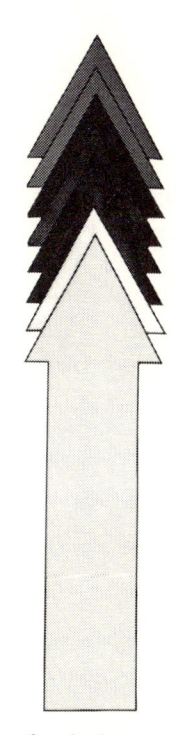

Seven New Age Economic Conditions

*There is a tide in the affairs of men
Which taken at the flood, leads on to fortune;
Omitted, all the voyage of their life,
Is bound in shallows and in miseries.*

— William Shakespeare

As the balance among natural resources, people in the labor force, media of exchange, and competition shifts, there are seven identifiable economic conditions produced to which we will be forced to respond in the New Age Economy. Remember that with a trend we have a choice of whether or not to respond, but with a prevailing condition the only choice is *how* to respond.

The seven conditions are:

- global and domestic competition
- targeted prosperity
- short shelf-life
- individual responsibility
- convulsive economy
- diversified financial services
- premium on human capital

These factors directly affect every aspect of our lives. Our preparation to respond to them plays a vital role in our future well-being both individually and also collectively as a nation.

CONDITION NUMBER 1: GLOBAL AND DOMESTIC COMPETITION

Perhaps the greatest force altering the complexion of the United States economy is competition—both at home and in an interconnected world. With the U.S. dollar being so strong in other countries, it is less expensive for Americans to buy imports than to buy their own products. Thus, we have a trade imbalance that threatens American companies' profits and stability. Almost every industry is affected and many jobs are at risk—especially those that are low-wage, standardized, and routine in task.

Because the United States is rapidly becoming integrated into a global economy, the labor force can be chosen from a broad worldwide base and not just from the U. S. labor base as has been characteristic of the past. The following are results of fierce domestic and global competition:

- Consumers demand more quality in their products than ever before and are losing their loyalty to "American-made" products if they are inferior to products manufactured in other countries.
- No longer can profit margins be expanded simply by adding to the price of a product or service.
- Severe competition causes industries to command fewer profits if productivity stays low.
- In the end, the American consumer wins productwise but is threatened economically.

Domestically, competition exists in all sectors. The age group of twenty to forty year olds is forcing competition for jobs not only among one another but also among people of over forty years of age. Increased availability of labor as well as decreased profits are causing many companies to offer early retirement packages to the middle-age and senior-age employees. Foreign companies are locating on American soil and offering still more competition on the domestic front.

However, in the bigger picture, the world economy is rapidly becoming interdependent with the United States becoming a major player in the global competition game. However, there is an imbalance in the wage base. The labor force in the U. S. commands much greater wages than similar workers of other countries. Because wage base becomes 50% to 70% of production cost, there is a major drive to get labor and production costs down. For example, the U. S. Department of Labor Statistics indicates that

Mexican wages are about forty to fifty cents per hour; in Bangladesh good workers can be obtained for sixteen cents per hour.[1] American industries, then, are contracting out low-wage, standardized-task jobs to such countries as Mexico, Taiwan, South Korea, and China while at the same time automating with robots to become more highly productive. This high level of competition for both price and quality takes away American jobs and puts them into other developing countries. A total of three million jobs have been displaced by global and domestic competition. Most of these displaced jobs are related to such Second Wave industries as steel, textiles, furniture, rubber, and petrochemicals.

Specific examples of competition clarify the U. S. worker's precarious position:

Household products

The toothpaste, laundry detergent, food product, personal care, paper product, and coffee product giant, known as Proctor and Gamble, once had a giant market share and a dominant position in the household products industry. New competitors are pushing Proctor and Gamble over on the supermarket shelves, and many of these companies are offering superior quality and competitively priced products. For the first time in 33 years, Proctor and Gamble announced its first decline in annual profits. On June 30, 1984, the company reported $809 million in earnings. By June 30, 1985, the company's earnings had declined to $640 million. Though the company is still very strong, competitive activity in its basic business is diluting its total market share.[2]

Retailing

The numbers of retail clothing stores are also growing by leaps and bounds and thereby squeezing profits. Montgomery Ward and Company is being restructured by its parent, Mobil Corporation, and will discontinue its catalog business. This will reduce Montgomery Ward's work force by about 5,000 employees nationwide by the end of 1986. This retailer's catalog operation was established in 1872, but that Second Wave operation, that earlier was so successful, is being discarded in management's efforts to become more productive, competitive, and efficient.

Houston-based Sakowitz closed its Dallas outlet due to several different problems "not the least of which was a squeeze of competition the day it opened," reported a *Dallas Times Herald* news article by Sally Bell.

Richard F. Mitchell, vice-chairman and chief executive officer of the Zale Corporation, speaking in 1985 to the financial executives division of the National Retail Merchants Association, stressed that successful retailing in the future will depend more on strategic thinking and management than on daily concentration on tactics and operation. During his speech he outlined five external factors that challenge retailers in the competition ahead:

- changing demographics
- market saturation resulting in too many stores within any one particular area
- promotional pricing forcing goods to be sold below profitable levels
- low productivity
- high cost of resources including capital, real estate for location of the store, energy, and labor costs.

These five areas outlined closely correspond to the balance of the economic factors which are discussed in Chapter 3. Because of the restructuring of these economic factors, we can see that a specific segment of the domestic economy is also directly affected.[3]

Automobiles

The U. S. portion of global automobile sales has been reduced by one-third since 1963. The U. S. is increasingly sharing its market for the automobile with Japan and European countries. During 1986, it is projected that U. S. automobile sales will decline while imports into the United States will increase substantially.[4] People buy foreign automobiles both for quality and for price. It has been reported that General Motors must reduce the person hours required to manufacture a car by approximately 78% in order to compete with Japanese manufacturers. This will be done through automation. General Motors, in addition, is beginning to retaliate in the global economy by structuring a new small car project in an unconventional way. In fact, when Roger Smith was interviewed by one of the big eight accounting firms, Deloitte, Haskins and Sells, he stated that when they laid out the new small car project in a conventional way, there was projected to be a negative return on investment. The old Second Wave methods of building a car were obviously not going to be profitable for General Motors any more. So General Motors came up with the

Saturn concept, which includes a whole new corporation, a whole new type of dealer franchise network, and a whole new kind of labor contract. General Motors, then, is becoming creative and is responding to the global and domestic competition of which we are all a part.[5]

Furniture

Much of the furniture manufacturing is being farmed out to other countries. One of the major countries for wood products is Mexico. The global economic complexion of the furnishings market is colored by the fact that the nation's first international furniture fair will be held in 1986. The event will be called the American International Furniture Fair. Manufacturers from Italy, France, Germany, England, and Canada will be participating along with other countries.[6] International competition will cause the furniture industry in America to suffer just as other industries are competing at this point.

Stock options trading

Even the nation's securities exchanges have been involved in competition. The New York Stock Exchange, the American Stock Exchange, the Chicago Board Options Exchange, and the Pacific Stock Exchange all now offer options on selected over-the-counter stocks.[7] The Securities and Exchange Commission in the past has allocated stock options to different exchanges. However, in April of 1985 it decided to allow all the exchanges to sell, in some cases, the very same options.

Airlines

The airline industry became involved in sweeping competition when that industry was deregulated seven years ago. Today the airline industry is involved in fierce, and often bitter, competition between major air carriers of the world. Many airlines are simply challenging themselves to survive. The fare wars and other competitive moves are driving some airlines out of business. Frank Borman, former chairman of Eastern Airlines, sees that other buyouts and mergers will change the landscape of the entire airline industry. He feels that, eventually, there will be approximately six full-service, large airlines that will serve major U.S. markets.

Since 1978, 119 airlines have quit the business. The fierce competitiveness is not only causing pricing wars but is also causing questioned safety standards. The year 1985 holds the record for being the worst year for civilian aviation deaths in the history of flying. The problem is not only in the United States; problems have also occurred with a major Japanese airline. Air disasters, price wars, and loss of human lives are causing close attention to be paid to the deregulated airline industry today.[8]

Broadcasting

The major networks, NBC, CBS, and ABC, are not only competitors with one another, but they are losing viewers to cable, video cassette recorders, and to other independent, entrepreneurial stations that are springing up all over the country. At one time, most shows would have had to attract 30% of the viewers to be seen as successful; however, if a show attracts 21% of the viewing audience, it is considered successful in today's viewing market.[9]

Public television is also competing with the major networks. In an effort to survive and compete in the years ahead, many public television networks are offering a step toward commercialism which they entitle "enhanced underwriting messages." These messages will allow more than company identification for program sponsors. In addition, those companies who sponsor programs will be able to provide more information about themselves for additional fees.[10]

Radio stations are in fierce competition in their metropolitan areas. All broadcasting stations are beginning to identify a specific audience and are matching that audience up with specific advertisers in order to survive.

Banking industry

Banks and savings institutions have entered into a new era of financial services. Such marketing powerhouses as Sears, K-Mart, and Merrill Lynch have set themselves up as intruders into a world once safely sheltered for traditional financial institutions. These "financial bizarres ... have attracted thousands of bank (and S&L) customers with lucrative new services." (*Time*, December 3, 1984.) Deregulation and increased competition have forced the traditional financial institutions into profit pressures, creative new products, and into strong emphasis on marketing. Why? According to the *Time* article mentioned above: "bankers and 'bank-like institutions' now face their most strenuous survival test since the Great Depression." [11]

Because banks through deregulation have been given more power to compete, many banks are failing as a result of the recession of 1982, oil and real estate price declines, weakness in many of their investments, and poor management. In 1984, eighty-one banks collapsed. In 1985, approximately 120 banks failed.[12] Consumers are beginning to question America's banking system and the competition in which it is involved. In 1984, a poll taken for *The American Banker* found that 36% of people surveyed said their faith in banks had fallen. In a Gallup poll, people who had a high degree of faith in banking dropped from 60% in 1979 to 51% in 1983.[13]

On the domestic front, Federal Reserve Chairman Paul Volcker has stated that he will back interstate banking which, then, will fuel more competition among banks.[14] In addition to interstate banking, which will eventually be a national banking system, there has been a tremendous increase in the placement of foreign agencies in the United States.

In fact, for the first time in Texas history, foreign banks can establish agency offices in the cities of Dallas and Houston. These foreign agency banks can now borrow and lend money within the state of Texas. They can conduct specific foreign transactions, and they can issue letters of credit. However, they may not collect deposits. Industry analysts feel that to attract attention these foreign agency offices will lend money at lower interest rates than Texas banks. Therefore, they will run head-on, direct competition with the state banking system.[15] This will then cause further fallout among Texas banks and cause a hard look at restructuring, operations, strategic marketing, and management of the Texas banking system. This will probably be a trend throughout the United States.

Due to domestic and international competition, eventually America's banking system will probably be dominated by a few strong global banks. The expansion will take place into a generalized financial service industry, and the banking system, as we know it, will not be recognized as it is today.

Textiles

Textile employment in the United States, according to the American Textile Manufacturers Institute, is at the lowest level in American history. Approximately 104,000 jobs were lost between August 1984 and September 1985. Seventy-one percent of all jobs lost in U. S. manufacturing from September 1984 to September

1985 were lost in the textile industry. Major competitors are Hong Kong, Taiwan, and ten other Far East suppliers.

Massachusetts-based Data Resources, Inc. has conducted a study and projects that by 1990, 80% of the United States apparel market will be accounted for by imports. This tremendous loss of domestic textile industry predicts that 947,000 jobs will be lost in the textile and apparel industries by 1990 and that 943,000 jobs will be lost in other industries that will supply and connect to the apparel industry.[16]

Of course, the American consumer and the retail industry in America profits from this situation because of price and quality of product. The losers in this competitive ripple effect are the apparel and textile industries based in America, as well as all the suppliers to the American-made product.

Steel

Largely a Second Wave industry and a supplier of materials to Second Wave industries, the world's steel production has shifted from the United States to other countries. By 1980, 15% of the world's steel-making capacity was housed in developing countries. Brazil and the Soviet Union hold the largest iron ore reserves in the world, and by 1977 Brazil had become the world's eighth largest steel producer. Mexico followed behind as the tenth largest, and Korea and Taiwan produced 20 million tons of raw steel by 1985. This is having a devastating effect on America's steel industry. Many plants are closing; many people are losing their jobs. Because of these competitive efforts, it is less expensive to import steel from other countries than it is to manufacture it with high labor costs in the United States.[17]

Communications

Since its breakup in January 1984, American Telephone and Telegraph is beginning to feel the pain of sudden competition. By 1986, the company planned to end the jobs of 24,000 workers from its Information Systems unit. Even though AT&T is beginning to feel the sting of competition, it continues to be *the* competition in the long distance telephone market with 80% of the market share.[18] Although it has approximately twelve major competitors, these competitors, at this point, make up about 20% of the total market share. It is predicted that AT&T will go head-on eventually with IBM in a computer battle. So, competition will stiffen now that AT&T is freed from specific restrictions and regulations and has unbundled its services. AT&T can now become a viable force in the highly competitive computer and communications industry. Many of the smaller high-tech companies, computer manufacturers, software companies, and other computer-related companies will fall victim to competition due to increased power of IBM and of AT&T in this global market.

Health care

The golden years of health care are disappearing. The industry, out of necessity, is borrowing long-used sales survival techniques from the business sector. With Medicare fee limitations to hospitals since 1983 and with domestic competition for patients at an all-time high, hospitals are beginning to offer special cut-rate fee packages on such services as obstetrics, face lifts, and cataract surgery.[19]

Competition in the health insurance industry among the traditional medical insurers, Health Maintenance Organizations (HMOs), and large hospital chains (who create their own insurance packages) will probably cut insurance and health care costs and will give the consumer more health care options. To compete, hospitals are consolidating and offering more diversified services. It is predicted that within the next ten years a few large national firms will provide greater than 50% of the medical care in the country.[20]

Doctors and dentists are also feeling the crunch of competition. Due to technological innovation, increasing numbers in the professions, and cost cutting of government and industry, many of these professionals will see a patient load decrease.[21] Because of these conditions, many medical professionals are already beginning to use creative selling and advertising techniques to promote their services. Some doctors are even beginning to make house calls again!

Conclusion

Still, global and domestic competition are taking toll on American markets. The individual worker will be directly affected by this changing pattern of U. S. foreign trade and a shift in domestic prosperity. For better or for worse, Americans must be prepared to respond to this vital issue in the New Age Economy.

CONDITION NUMBER 2: TARGETED PROSPERITY

Charles Dickens, in *A Tale of Two Cities,* conjectured: "It was the best of times. It was the worst of times." No statement has been truer of today's transition period into the New Age Economy. While some industries are thriving, others are barely surviving. This great unevenness in business conditions varies *among* industry units, *within* industries, and *among* geographical areas of the country; i.e., we see the economic conditions of targeted prosperity. However, there is a distinct pattern to the simultaneous boom and bust phenomenon now taking place.

Variation among industry units

The pre-industrial or First Wave industries of agriculture, mining, fishing, and timber are suffering setbacks due to surplus production and/or environmental constraints. Heavy machinery manufacturing, transportation, utilities, oil and gas, textiles, shoes, steel, rubber, and ship building — all representative of Second Wave or industrial society — are suffering declines in earnings and even losses due to competition, deregulation, or the fact that much work previously done in America is now being contracted to Third World developing industrial nations as was discussed in the competition section of this chapter.

Yet, while many industries are losing profits and people, other industries are excelling in productivity and growth. These industries include super computers, artificial intelligence, robotics, medical equipment, lasers, fiber optics, and telecommunications. These industries are distinctly those of the New Age Economy — information-based, knowledge-powered, and capital-intensive for research and development.[22]

Variation within industry units

Generalizations are always dangerous. Not all First and Second Wave industries are in bust status. Not all New Age industries are booming. Prosperity is definitely targeted even within industries.

Even though the oil drilling business is in a state of decline, some companies are doing well and continuing to reap lucrative rewards through strategic planning and timing in the energy business. For example, Robert T. Priddy, chief executive officer, sold his majority interest in Dual Drilling Company in 1980 when the oil business was peaking. That gave the company a source of capital to enter new drilling markets. The company is turning to development of international and offshore reserves for major oil companies. Through strategic planning, the company was able to survive a decline in the industry when as many as one-third of the 800 to 900 firms in the International Association of Drilling Contractors will become victims of the downturn in the oil drilling business.[23]

The value of American farmland has dropped by the greatest percentage since the Great Depression. American farmland's value has declined by 12%, and crops are selling for similar prices (in real dollars) as during the Great Depression.[24] Although it is admittedly difficult, some farmers are still profiting. Those farmers who are surviving have land and equipment paid for, no loans against their land, and low labor costs. Also, many farmers have land located in booming areas of the country and have sold their real estate to become instant multimillionaires.

At the opposite extreme, for example, the personal computer market boomed in 1984, but sales are now being cornered by a few computer powerhouses; once prominent computer companies have either been forced totally out of business or have been forced to restructure operations and to lay off people. During any growth period for new industry, normally much fallout of undercapitalized, small entrepreneurial companies occurs. They either merge, become targets for buyouts, or go out of business. This phenomenon is now active in the development of the many New Age industries that are emerging.

Variation within geographic areas

Regions of the country can even be correlated to industrial prosperity. For instance, portions of Texas, California, midwestern states, central states, and northwestern states can be tagged directly to agriculture. The economies of these states then suffer when agriculture in general suffers. Oil and gas drilling is a prominent industry in Alaska, Oklahoma, Louisiana, East and West Texas, and offshore in the Gulf of Mexico. Their economy, building, housing, and even the amount of groceries sold relate directly to the prosperity experienced in their major industry. The coal industry is correlated to the prosperity of West Virginia, Pennsylvania, and Wyoming. Areas of Massachusetts, California, and Texas are becoming prominent in the New Age economic industries — those that are specifically connected to high technology and information systems. Much entrepreneurial activity is taking place at this time, and their economies are doing well. Future research for solar energy will occur in many states which have much sun — California, Arizona, and Colorado. Tourism is a prosperous industry in many states. California, Texas, Florida, and Tennessee are targeting tourism as one of their major industries.

Populations tend to move toward prosperity. It is very obvious that the Third Wave industries concerning information, knowledge, high technology, tourism, and other service industries are attracting the larger population moves within the United States today. People from smokestack, coal, oil, and agricultural areas are moving into the regions that are supportive of New Age industries. Thus, prosperity can even be traced to specific regions.

The ripple effect

All support services of the basic boom/bust industries feel the ripple of either prosperity or decline. For example, housing foreclosures in 1983 can be directly targeted to First and Second Wave industries. Most of the delinquencies that went all the way to foreclosure for homes were in areas where local economies are tied to oil and gas, agriculture, lumber, and steel because pressures from these industries caused people to be unable to make their house payments. Employment decline in these major industries caused people to lose their homes. In 1985, specific areas of the country were finding prices of real estate plummeting due to poor performance of First and Second Wave industries. For instance, in some once oil-rich locations, $300,000 condominiums could be purchased for somewhere between $180,000 and $200,000.

Banks serving the petroleum industry and agriculture are seeing troubled times. Many of these banks that had overextended themselves in energy loans are finding themselves being taken over by the Federal Depositors Insurance Corporation, reorganized, and absorbed by other banks. In fact, most bank troubles in 1984 and 1985 can be traced directly to loans to the petroleum and agriculture industries which failed to repay loans.[25]

While many industrial support services are suffering, at the same time many support services are feeling untold prosperity. Consulting to telecommunication companies and entrepreneurial

Seven New Age Economic Conditions

ventures are at an all-time profitable high as is venture capital development to fund these fresh new growth companies.

Targeted prosperity, then, operates via a network of intricately connected industrial types, companies within industry, and sections of the country.

Crossing lines?

Some industries have chosen to move from Second Wave status to the New Age. General Motors, for example, is computerizing assembly lines and automobiles, developing creative labor union contracts, and diversifying into new products and services in an effort to cross into the New Age information economy. At the same time, some Second Wave industries other than General Motors have tried to raise capital, cut wages, and renegotiate labor contracts in order to keep doing what they have always done for the past thirty years. That type of thinking on the part of Second Wave industrial management can render a company extinct.

By appropriately responding to the economic conditions of targeted prosperity, Americans can choose whether to be richer or poorer. Americans, indeed, have the choice of whether to tag their career futures and their investment strategies to industries that are in poverty or to create opportunities for themselves by associating with those industries that are in good health.

CONDITION NUMBER 3: SHORT SHELF-LIFE

Characteristic of the New Age Economy will be rapid product/service cycling or short shelf-life. Products, social institutions, people, and career positions will come and go at a rapid rate. Fifty percent of the products available by the year 2000 have not been discovered yet. Forty-one firms on the Forbes 100 list in 1945 had disappeared by 1977. Most of the companies on today's Fortune 500 list did not exist in the 1920s.[26] The list for tomorrow is not yet known. However, many companies on the Fortune 500 list today will vanish by the year 2000. Most manual blue-collar jobs will be replaced by automation by the year 2010.[27]

As a result of short shelf-life, Americans will live in a society that will:

- promote early corporate retirement for the next twenty years
- provide no guarantees of job security
- bear testimony to increased job obsolescence

- accentuate speed of process for convenience and time savings
- witness massive new product development with a high degree of product failure.

Early retirement

An estimated 20% of companies are offering or contemplating offering early retirement programs due to mergers, takeovers, deregulation of various industries, and changing economic conditions.[28] There were 1,899 mergers in 1984 compared to 1,812 in 1983, and these mergers dictate the fact that some people must leave the organization.[29] Such companies as American Airlines, DuPont, Firestone Tire & Rubber, Atlantic Richfield, Phillips Petroleum, Owens-Illinois, Bank of America, and Texas Instruments have offered in the past, or are offering in the present, lucrative early retirement packages. For some people this "early out" is a dream come true. For others, it is a frightening experience at a time when they are too old to find other equal opportunities and are too young to go into retirement. Other employees report mixed emotions: they cannot afford financially to retire early, but they are afraid that eventually their jobs will disappear and they will be forced to leave anyway without the incentive of early retirement.

People who planned to work fifteen more years are finding their plans challenged in their midyears, when they had always felt life would be easier—not harder and more frustrating.

No guarantees of job security

Even for those people who founded their own companies, job security at that company is not always assured. Personality problems, management conflicts, buyouts, mergers, and stockholder dissension after a company goes public can cause top-level executives to topple from their high-level posts.

Employees of once booming companies can suffer job loss. Apple Computer, the symbol of the personal computer's rapid growth in the early 1980s, dismissed 21% of its work force in 1985 due to a downturn in the personal computer market and tremendous competition among corporate computer giants. The company, founded in 1978, peaked and was forced into restructure within a seven-year period.[30] Approximately 20,000 total workers have been idled in the personal computer and semiconductor industries since the fall of 1984.[31] In the energy industry alone, Tulsa, Oklahoma, reports 1,200 workers, among them 80–90% white-collar workers, have lost their jobs between December 1983 and December 1984 due to the downturn in energy production.[32] So, once booming companies and industries can suffer very rapid rise and fall.

Midlevel management ranks are shrinking drastically in even well-managed companies. Automation and rearranged hierarchies are having impact on midlevel positions ranging from $25,000 to $80,000 salary levels. Many midlevel managers who suffer job loss will never replace their salary again—especially those who command $60,000 or more annually, not including corporate benefits. In 1983, unemployment among management and administration in non-farm-related industries reached the highest level since World War II—according to the U. S. Bureau of Labor Statistics.[33]

Increased career obsolescence

A person's career position will change in responsibility and technology approximately every five years. Until the 1960s, radical changes might not have occurred during a person's total career lifetime. Many people could expect to go to work in their twenties and work to age sixty-five with very little to learn new. Now all this has changed. Some jobs will be restructured every six months—especially those that are technology related.

Specific jobs will be outmoded by technology by the year 2000. Among those targeted for demise are machinists, packers, typists, mailroom clerks, draftspeople, bank clerks, small farm workers, grocery checkers—and all others that can be replaced by more productive technology. Retraining for new jobs will be an essential ingredient for career survival.[34]

Speed of process

Because time will be a great commodity in the New Age Economy, production speed will have more value placed on it. Turnaround per product from inception to market shelf will be greatly reduced due to consumer demand and competition.

To cite a few examples where speed is being enhanced:

- McDonnell Douglas and other aircraft firms are developing an ultrasonic airliner that cruises at 5,000 miles per hour—those airliners will be able to go back and forth from Asia in the same day.[35]

- To speed table service and turnover, the restaurant waiter will soon be able to key in an order and have it electronically transmitted to the kitchen.[36]
- For faster infection diagnosis, a machine is coming out that will spot such diseases as strep throat, meningitis, and hepatitis. Diagnosis can be made in minutes rather than in hours as the system is now.[37]
- Computers can be programmed via voice mode input to save writing a computer program as in the past.[38]

All these innovations plus many more will increase speed and production and rescue more of the New Age Economy's most valuable resource — time.

New product development/failure

"In 1982 over 1,500 products were introduced in the categories of food and health and beauty aids alone," says *SME Digest*.[39] Rising along with new products introduced is also the number of product failures.

From June to August 1985, profits of computer makers fell almost 30%. Sales of personal computers for the home dropped another 10% in 1985.[40] Today's computers will be obsolete soon, replaced by easier to use, faster, and smarter machines.

Thus, we see that product introduction and failure will take place at blinding speed and will continually change American lifestyle over the next thirty-year period.

CONDITION NUMBER 4: INDIVIDUAL RESPONSIBILITY

Since the basic economic unit of the New Age Economy is the individual, there will be an economic condition of individual responsibility; i.e., the individual must plan to take total responsibility for his career, finances, and lifestyle planning.

The independent thinker is rewarded in corporations today. In fact, members of the baby boom generation emphasize two desired freedoms on the job — freedom to be creative and to have corporate leadership's ear with freedom of schedule. The majority of workers who are twenty-four to forty years old respond better when allowed freedom of movement and do not respond well to authoritative management.

People are seeking independence more than ever before. Record numbers of entrepreneurs are in the business world today. These achievement-oriented, self-managed people want to be their own bosses — to be in charge of their own destinies. They leave perceived-to-be secure positions for high-risk opportunities — the opportunity to be individually responsible.

Most everyone is really self-employed even though they might work for a corporation, for there is no guarantee of security anywhere today. Leadership changes, economic problems, mergers and acquisitions may cause a worker of several years' tenure to become unemployed. In the end, the employee must always look out for his own well-being.[41] That has become a fact of corporate and government life in the New Age Economy.

Corporations and the United States government are promoting independence by helping people to help themselves financially. Many corporations are terminating pension plans to which the company solely contributes and are replacing those benefits with plans to which employees contribute — perhaps with tax breaks.[42]

The tax laws favor individual retirement accounts and several other retirement plans. These efforts are being made to help working people become independent in old age. By the year 2010, there will be two workers to support every one worker on Social Security. That could put a strain on the system and cause the percentage of income replaced by Social Security to be much less for the baby boom population than for today's retiree.

Even married people need to be self-sufficient financially. With 50–60% of marriages ending in divorce, a majority of married people must strike out on their own again — often after a painful splitting of property. Stanford University statistics show that the average lifestyle of the woman who is the victim of divorce goes down 73% in the year after her divorce. The lifestyle of the male goes up 42% during that same period.[43]

With more marriages ending in divorce and with more people living longer — even twenty years longer in the twenty-first century than in the twentieth century — there will be more diversified lifestyles. Either through personal choice or through circumstances beyond one's control, people will be single, single parents, widowed, married, living alone, living in groups of two or more, and sharing dwellings bound only by legal contract — just to name a few of the varied lifestyles. Because of this lack of permanency in lifestyle, the individually responsible individual will be more optimistic and emotionally stable in the New Age Economy.

Convulsive Economy

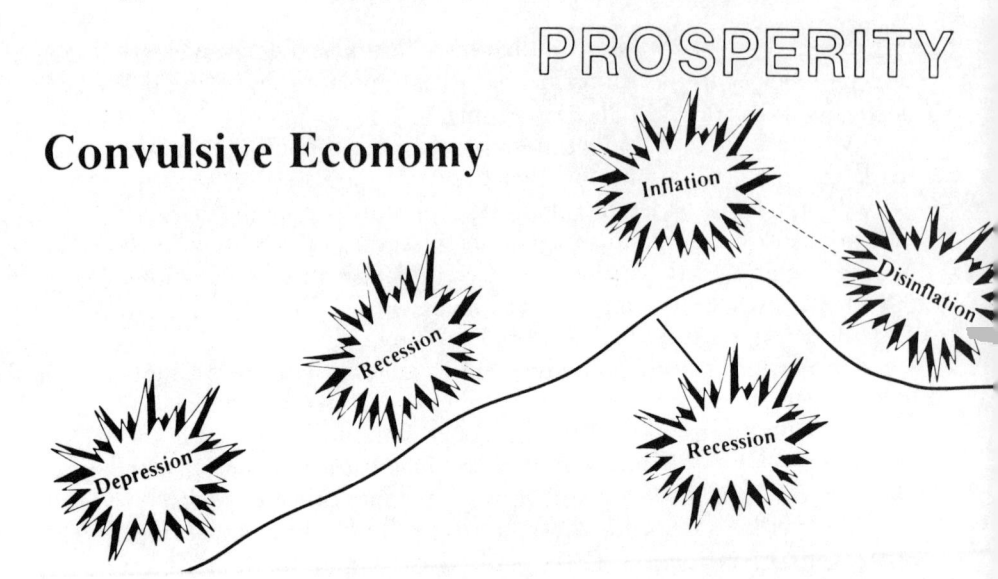

PROSPERITY

Inflation

Disinflation

Recession

Recession

Depression

CONDITION NUMBER 5: CONVULSIVE ECONOMY

The economy is in a schizophrenic mode. Although the conditions are frightening, they will eventually level out and mature if we can, indeed, move as a nation into the New Age Economy. However, there are some things we have to fix first.

News headlines in 1985 indicated that we became a debtor nation for the first time since 1914.[44] In the years since we bought and paid for our freedom from Great Britain, we were a nation generally out of debt for the most part. It took almost 200 years to build a sound economy, and it took us two and one-half years to get back into debt. Now we owe foreigners more than they owe us. They have invested in our farmland and in many other investments such as bonds. This means that interest and other types of payments that could be paid to Americans and be used to help our corporations and run our U.S. government are not going to be there anymore. They are being paid out to foreign nations.

Another problem we have to solve in our convulsive economy is the import-export deficit. This means that we are now bringing into our country more than we are exporting. That deficit exceeded $120 billion at the end of 1985. Many jobs will be replaced with low-cost labor of other countries. We have already lost three million jobs due to the import-export deficit. Many more jobs will probably be lost before the situation improves.

There are two other problems which we have to solve before the economy will quit being convulsive. One problem is the budget deficit. The budget deficit approximated $200 billion by the end of 1985. It is projected to go down somewhat by 1988. Another problem that is causing convulsiveness in the economy is the huge international debt structure. A great percentage of the loans out by major banks today are to foreign countries. Five times the assets of America's ten largest banks were on loan to Latin American countries in 1982.[45]

A convulsive economy can be fixed. It is going to take belt-tightening. It is going to take some sacrifice by all of us working together as a nation. Then, we can move into another economy that will be bigger and better and more stable than any civilization has ever known.

CONDITION NUMBER 6: DIVERSIFIED FINANCIAL SERVICES

Financial services are diversifying at a rapid rate. Eventually, in about ten to twenty years, all financial services will be concentrated in the hands of a few big corporations. Consumers will decide which of these financial organizations will survive.

In the future, bankers will sell insurance and will have the right to sell stocks and other financial services. Sears Roebuck and other major retailers will be in diversified financial activities. Major savings and loan and brokerage firms will also be diversified. Banks, savings and loans, brokerage firms, and all other services of financial character will lose their individual identities and will be merged into industries that will be tagged "financial services."

During the diversification and deregulation of the financial services industry, the consumer will be confused. Many different accounts will be offered, and they will be tailored to individual needs. In fact, today many financial institutions can offer in excess of 250 different account possibilities to the customer. So, in the future, we will find that financial services will be very diversified and will be constructed for convenience and cost savings to the institution and to the customer. The consumer will decide which companies in the financial services industry will survive. There will probably be five to ten major financial servants who will serve the American consumer in approximately fifteen to twenty years.

CONDITION NUMBER 7: PREMIUM ON HUMAN CAPITAL

In the New Age Economy there will be a premium on human capital. This seems contradictory to the fact that robots and computers will be in heavy use to replace repetitive activity. For example, as General Motors reduces production time on its average automobile in order to compete with Japanese production and pricing, it must have a worker who does not talk, does not take lunch breaks, and does not have sick days. The result of this need will be to replace many people with robots. Thus, anyone who does not do anything unique or who cannot make a unique contribution to the work force will be replaced and displaced by robots and other automation processes. Then we will have more consistent productivity.

However, those people who have significant *know how* and *know who* in this environment will be able to name their price in the work place. In other words, those people who have the ability to manipulate information, lead people, and foster networks, as well as those people who are specialized in needed fields, will prosper in the New Age Economy. There will be much money paid for those talents. Corporations will be employee-driven, and specialized leadership will be a requirement.

Seven Conditions: Opportunities for Prosperity

These seven conditions are already being evidenced today and will mature over the next thirty-year period. Those people who anticipate these conditions and make plans to respond to these conditions in a positive way will reap untold prosperity in the New Age Economy.

A new frontier lies before us. We are living in the most exciting time of American history. We have a chance to conquer new frontiers, we have a chance to renew America's strength, and again have the opportunity to dream.

Summary:
1. During the next twenty to thirty years, there will be at least seven economic conditions to which we will respond.
2. Global and domestic competition affects the American work force by decreasing availability of jobs and by cutting profits while, at the same time, favoring better consumer prices.
3. There will be simultaneous boom and bust among industries, within industry groups,

Seven New Age Economic Conditions 57

and among sections of America.
4. Products and people will have a shorter shelf-life than ever before.
5. Economic conditions favor the individual who assumes individual responsibility.
6. The economy will be in an up-and-down, convulsive mode for several years hence because of trade imbalance, budget deficits, high international and consumer debt, and financial services deregulation.
7. Due to deregulation of financial services and merging of many financial industries, all institutions, as we knew them in the 1950s through the 1970s, will take on a new identity. The ability to survive competition, maintain management quality, and meet consumer needs will help determine the survivors.
8. Those people who know how to manage the New Age employee, funnel information into specialized knowledge, and who understand the New Age Economy, will be in great demand in the work place.

PART THREE

Strategies for Prosperity in the 1980s, 1990s, and Beyond

Chapter 5

Power Positioning: Lessons Of Survival And Prosperity From Great Corporations

Power is the force that shapes destiny.
—Author

With the seven economic conditions partially in place today, we are feeling the need to respond appropriately. Great lessons can be learned from what corporations are doing to survive and prosper under these challenging circumstances. Some organizations are merging and venturing into joint efforts while others are finding a narrower niche from which to market their services. In responding to these economic conditions, corporate strategies may fall under one or more of the following five categories.

1. Become big, powerful, unique
2. Practice long-range planning
3. Pool corporate resources
4. Pare overhead for sounder capital base
5. Develop extended human resource orientation

Under the first category, we find several mergers especially of large oil companies: Superior Oil Company/Mobil Oil Company, Gulf/Chevron Corporations, Getty Oil/Texaco. Philip Morris is merging with General Foods to become the nation's largest consumer products company. While mergers create strength from the standpoint of magnitude in the face of competition, other corporations are diversifying for strength and going into other services. Not only are they becoming bigger, they also are finding more to offer. For instance, General Motors has bought Hughes Aircraft, a high-tech engineering and manufacturing company. General Motors also purchased Electronic Data Systems for diversification into computer applications and financial services.[1]

Other companies are combating competition by finding a specific niche that has never been served before or by providing better service in an established niche. For example, flying pebbles formerly caused "pings" in automobile windshields, and as a result auto owners had to replace the total windshield. A company called Glass Savers, Inc. came up with a way to service these problems without having to replace the total windshield — thus saving insurance money or out-of-pocket expense. That organization is now franchising across the United States and overseas because it found its niche.[2] Another successful example is Wang Laboratories, which discovered a need in the word processing field and dominated it. Wang is now planning to expand its position and to become a leader in the office automation market. Recently, it formed an alliance with InteCom and plans to develop and market products with features that combine telecommunications and the computer.[3]

No longer can corporations plan for a mere one, two, or even five years hence. In order to compete internationally with companies that are conducting extremely detailed research into the future, organizations today are forming pools with departments of physics, biology, engineering, chemistry, and other college areas in order to fund long-range research and development. For example, Sun Exploration and Production Company will build a $35 million technology center next to the University of Texas at Dallas in order to pursue future development and complementary academic work. Long-range planning is no longer a luxury. In the past, many executives felt they did not have time for this type of planning. Now there is no alternative. In order to survive in our rapidly changing world, corporations must plan for ten, twenty, thirty years down the road.[4]

Some companies are choosing neither to merge nor to purchase other companies, but to form joint ventures in order to gain more strength. They will pull on the positive, marketable strengths of each organization. Usually two organizations will form a joint venture and perhaps come up with a third company with members of the two organizers sitting on the board. GTE Telenet of the

United States has formed a joint venture with Intec and Sumitomo Corporation of Japan. Their joint venture will be an electronic messaging service headquartered in Japan.

ABC is forming a joint venture with Hurst Corporation to develop new cable programming services. N. V. Phillips and AT&T will form an association to provide quick expansion abroad for AT&T services as well as some of the services that N. V. Phillips can offer. In addition, they will develop new products. Three companies — Sears Roebuck, CBS, and IBM — have formed Trintex to develop videotext products which probably will relate to shopping and financial services. Also, Western Union, airplanes, and ground transportation will be used to deliver videotapes to various news stations in a new experiment for pooled resources. NBC and fourteen of its Texas affiliates are beginning an experimental program to air news stories in an effort to improve the news coverage of the total state of Texas. After the news stories are delivered via various transportation techniques, the stories will be sent by satellite to each participating station. This is part of an experiment testing out a long-range plan to gain competitive advantage over stations that do not have such service.[5]

Due to falling oil prices, many United States oil corporations are consolidating with other companies to increase capital strength. Many of these companies took on debt to expand into non-energy areas. Survivors of this industry will be those that have the financial strength and a good cash position. These strong companies will be able to buy out the weak ones. Corporations are now working to reduce their debt, especially in the face of falling oil prices and competition. The strong will survive. The weak will be absorbed.

Again another example is the buyout of Electronic Data Systems by General Motors. This was an effort to bring state-of-the-art factory automation to plants. Accounting firms also are beginning to feel the crunch of competition, and it is predicted that some of these firms — even the larger firms — will merge in order to provide better and more diversified services to clients. Many small accounting firms that were formed simply for accounting purposes find that it is no longer enough to offer just these services. They have been forced to merge with other firms to expand their services. So we see that corporations are running lean, reducing debt, reducing the number of people in their work force either through attrition, early retirement packages or layoffs, and are automating. In other words, they are getting ready for a long, hard race and are paring their forces in order to run rapidly, make quick decisions, respond to change promptly and to win in the competition race.

In the last category we find that companies who are surviving in this New Age are those who realize the value of their employees and their customers, i.e., they are becoming more human-resource oriented. General Motors is trying a New Age management philosophy and feels very successful in its use. It allows employees to think more for themselves and to introduce new ideas into the system. They are pushing responsibility to levels lower than middle management. They are asking their people to take on more authority. The company itself, though a corporate giant, is breaking itself down into areas that can become more entrepreneurial and can have the vivacity and positive growth of smaller growth organizations.[6]

Reaction of the consuming public in 1985 to the Coca-Cola experiment caused the giant company to reverse a decision and bring back the old formula of the original Coke. This is a prime example of a company responding to a majority of its consumers. In the New Age, we will see more and more consumer-driven companies as well as employee-driven organizations. Corporations will be forced to listen to their customers and to their people. Those who do will have a tremendous chance to prosper under these seven economic conditions. A recent Federal Reserve Bank of Atlanta study of twenty-one high-performing companies in the Southeast summarizes well these five lessons of corporate survival and prosperity. The study found that there were four commonalities of high performing corporations.

- The companies were creative; in fact, innovation was emphasized.
- The corporations remained lean and flexible through an entrepreneurial management style; employees were encouraged to take risks.
- Employees were viewed as associates — very valuable assets. There was no "we/they" attitude of employees versus management.
- The companies continued to have a long-range marketing strategy that focused on comparative advantages of the company. Marketing was considered very important to the organization.[7]

Through observation of all the tactics and techniques that these companies are using in the face of competition, as well as the extensive review of research, it seems that corporations are practicing *power positioning*. Note that we did not say that they are acquiring a power position because that defines a static marketplace. They are dynamic and continuing to position themselves for power. Thus we use a more active phrase to describe these corporations' activities: *power positioning*.

The lessons to be learned for individuals can come when people make application of these corporate activities in their personal lives. It seems that in the New Age if you, as an individual, know how to properly proportion your time into managing three life resources, you will hold the secrets to prosperity. If you know how to manage yourself, people, and money in the New Age, and if you can properly apply your proven techniques, then you can prosper beyond your comprehension.

However, knowing these techniques is not enough. You must make application at the proper place and at the proper time. If enough people would apply these principles and would learn to live triumphantly in the New Age, then we could hopefully avert what the Kondratieff Wave (mentioned in Chapter 2) predicts will occur: another economic collapse.

Below are listed the five lessons from great organizations that we have discussed. The lessons have been transferred into five strategies that individuals can apply for success in the New Age. Note that these individual strategies all involve the management of either self, people, or money.

Corporate Strategies	*Individual Strategies*
Corporations are becoming bigger, more powerful, more diversified.	DECLARE YOUR INDEPENDENCE
Companies are engaging in more long-range planning.	ANTICIPATE TOMORROW'S BUSINESS WORLD
Companies are pooling their efforts into joint ventures.	DEVELOP RESOURCE CONNECTORS
Corporations are paring down and becoming lean to form a sound capital base in order to run faster in the competition race.	PREPARE FOR PREDICTABLE UNCERTAINTY
Organizations are becoming more human-resource oriented.	RELEASE YOURSELF TO RELATE

These five strategies must be combined; no one application used in isolation will necessarily offer prosperity. The following five chapters provide suggestions for implementation of these concepts in your lifestyle planning for the New Age Economy.

Summary:
1. Individuals can learn valuable lessons by observing what the great corporations are doing in response to the seven economic conditions.
2. People who know how to prioritize their time into the management of three life resources — self, people, and money — will begin to know the secrets of prosperity in the New Age.
3. Five individual strategies for prosperity can be drawn from the business world's five lessons of survival.

Chapter 6

Declare Your Independence

A master of his craft shall stand before kings.
— Proverbs 22:29
(paraphrased)

John S., age fifty-five, has worked for his corporation for years. He began as a staff member thirty years ago just after graduating from college. After receiving several promotions and healthy pay raises, he had finally built his lifestyle into that which met most of his personal and income goals. John has two children—one a freshman and the other a senior in college. His work pressures are heavy, but John copes well and manages to have a good family and social life. Two years ago, however, his corporation began to lose market share of its product line to foreign competition. Today, in order to prevent more losses, the corporation's stockholders sold out to a major and powerful competitor. John realizes that after the two companies merge, his position may be in jeopardy. He could very well be offered a lucrative early retirement package. He feels that if he were to decline this offer, he might not have a position with the company any longer.

This situation presents a great dilemma in John's life. He had fully planned to work at his company until age sixty-five. He and his wife were able to start saving for retirement just five years ago. With two children in college, there continues to be a drain on family resources. Even the lucrative early retirement package will not sustain the family as would his present salary. Besides, John does not know what to do for a career alternative at his age. Just at the time of his life that John had anticipated would be secure and relatively carefree, he has been confronted with one of his greatest financial and career challenges. He never dreamed that this would happen to him.

Samantha T., age thirty-five, grew up in a small Southern town. She was always very popular in high school and was chosen by her senior class as "Most Likely to Succeed." During her sophomore year in college she met Fred, the man of her dreams, and they were married the following summer. Life became very busy, and finances became tight. Samantha quit college to go to work while Fred continued his education. By age 26, Fred had received his college degree and had embarked on a promising marketing career. Samantha intended to finish school but opted to begin a family instead. As the demands of family life coupled with her career as a bank auditing assistant began to pressure her, she never found time to complete her education. However, Samantha had a good life financially. Family income exceeded $50,000 per year, and she and Fred were able to finance a beautiful home with a swimming pool.

Seven months ago, Samantha received the shock of her life — Fred took her to dinner to ask her for a divorce. After fourteen years of marriage, he had found someone else — someone with whom he could better relate, someone who made him feel like "Superman."

Today Samantha's life has changed drastically. She has had to sell the house because she could not afford the upkeep. Family income dropped in excess of 50%, and her lifestyle has become totally different as a one-income single parent with a minimal additional income from child support payments. Samantha is bitter. She is angry — mostly at herself. She spends hours contemplating what went wrong. She feels as if she is a victim of circumstances beyond her control.

John S. and Samantha T. are becoming typical Americans — those who feel victimized by rapid corporate and family changes and puzzled by how to resolve their attitude to accept a lifestyle much different from that of which they had dreamed. John is a victim of competition and Samantha of short marital shelf-life and a convulsive family economy. Both have found that there is a need for individual responsibility. Three of the seven heretofore cited economic conditions are working in their lives today.

There is good news for John and Samantha, however. They may feel victimized, but in reality they could have been victors through a little long-range planning. Because they are already in their situations, they must work hard to win over adversity, but it can be done.

A better way, though, would have been for John and Samantha to have anticipated these conditions and to have prepared in advance.

We can learn valuable lessons from these two people: dependency, both psychological and financial, can be devastating. So as a first step to power positioning, become an *indipreneur*, i.e.,

DECLARE YOUR INDEPENDENCE.

Declaring your independence does not mean that you should quit your job or become a family runaway. But it does mean that you can take necessary steps to mentally, emotionally, and financially go into business with yourself. You then regard yourself as a small independent business unit (an indipreneurship) with your employer, family, church, friends, and other systems of interaction as your clients.

Note that I said, "Go into business *with* yourself," not *for* yourself. There is a vast difference between the two phrases. When you go into business *for* yourself, that almost assures selfish motives, i.e., a separation from business and personal issues of importance with pursuit of your own happiness first. But by going into business *with* yourself, you establish a partnership with yourself. And, almost without fail, partnerships are more powerful and objective than sole proprietorships. You continue to be a team player in your business, family, and social life, but you have taken precautions to insulate yourself from possibly falling victim to circumstances beyond your control. As an indipreneur you realize that all of life's circumstances cannot be controlled, but, as long as you are mentally alert, you can control your *responses* to those circumstances.

In order for a partnership to be successful, it must at least do the following:

- be adequately capitalized
- develop a marketable product line
- market test the products

- develop customers and clients
- package the product for sale to its market
- promote the product line, and
- share information with similar businesses through associations and professional networks in order to increase knowledge and performance.

These same principles can be transferred from the business world to your own indipreneurship. Here's how to make that transition:

Steps to a Successful Business Partnership	*Steps to a Successful Indipreneurship*
Be adequately capitalized	Create a strong savings and investment program
Develop a marketable product line	Find your niche
Market test the products	Perfect your special, unique marketable skills
Develop customers and clients	Create a market for your skills clusters
Package the product for sale to its market	Package yourself for personal impact
Promote the product line	Practice creative self-promotion techniques
Share information with similar businesses through associations and professional networks in order to increase knowledge and performance	Be a team player

Let's now examine these seven steps to independence in the New Age.

CREATE A STRONG INVESTMENT AND SAVINGS PROGRAM

By having a strong investment and savings program, you develop a cushion of security. In turn, you buy yourself freedom. By age forty it is a good idea to have assets other than your home, auto, and personal possessions that could sustain you for one year without working. By age fifty-five, it would be helpful to be able to maintain your lifestyle supported only by part-time work or ideally by no work at all.

When you have cushioned yourself for financial freedom, you then have the availability of more choices in your life. You feel that you work for an employer because you wish, not because you must. You feel less financial and emotional strain on the family unit, and you are independent to be more creative, to take more risks, to be more of what you are designed to be.

In Chapter 9, I discuss the development of financial freedom in more detail. Because of the importance of money in power positioning, I have developed the management and use of it into a strategy all its own.

FIND YOUR NICHE

Housed in the National Archives Building in Washington, D.C. are three documents that are very precious to the American people: our Declaration of Independence, our Constitution, and our Bill of Rights. Each of these documents is kept in a helium-filled glass case and lowered seventy feet below ground level every night to protect them against some disaster that might occur. When I heard about this process, I immediately began to think: "Why do we go to such lengths to protect these documents? I can buy a copy of any one of these instruments in a dime store for less than two dollars." As I thought about it more and more, I began to realize that these documents are so valuable because they are the originals. And a copy is never as good a quality as an original. So if we lost these documents, we would lose a real part of our American heritage that could never be replaced.

You, too, are an original. In fact, when the chromosomes of your mother united with the chromosomes of your father, the possibility of your becoming who you are was in excess of one in eight million. I firmly believe that God did not create you to be like everybody else, but that God designed you to make a difference.

To find what that difference is that you will make takes intense self-exploration. By looking hard enough and long enough, you can identify marketable skills clusters, which I will define as a number of skills that when grouped together form your unique talent or become the tools by which you will make your unique contribution to the world.

It is not a specific skill that makes you unique, but a combination of skills in specific proportions that defines your uniqueness. Also, it is important to define your skills clusters rather than label yourself by a position, for example, computer programmer. Because of the economic condition of short shelf-life of career positions as we know them today, you must be able to transfer skills into different career functions as they evolve. Let's expand our example of the computer programmer. To excel in this position takes a person highly skilled in assessment, analysis, diagnosis, evaluation, synthesis, detail observation, problem solution, abstract thinking, visualization, and patience—just to name a few. A person with a grouping of these skills would probably be a very good computer programmer. However, these same combinations lend themselves to such fields as engineering, accounting, and several aspects of scientific research. For one to excel in these fields would simply take the motivation to acquire additional knowledge and perhaps even additional college degrees.

Niche may sometimes be identified as a "calling." Rather than be called to a specific vocation in the New Age, you will be compelled to identify skills and motives then find an outlet for them. Just last week, Joe R. came up to me after a seminar and questioned, "I know we all have a niche, but how do we find it?" I told Joe what has been one of the most helpful indicators for me in finding my own niche. "Joe," I said, "think back to your childhood because when you were a child you dreamed without barriers and restrictions. You were more in tune with yourself as a child than perhaps you are now since adults are fenced in by standards of performance and by real or imagined expectations. What did you want to be when you grew up? You didn't have to have a career label. Why did you want to become that? How did you arrive at your decision? Was it because of expectations of parents, modeling after a specific adult hero, or because you really wanted to play a certain role in life for your very own reasons? If your own reasons were involved, then you should determine your motives."

Joe thought about my series of questions for a while and then came back to me and said, "You know, when I was a child I always wanted to be a veterinarian—not because my parents expected it of me or because I modeled after a veterinarian hero, but really because I loved animals, the freedom to move about that veterinarians seem to have (at least they are not tied to a desk), and because they are their own bosses. Come to think of it, after analyzing my motives, there are other professions that allow these same qualities. I don't necessarily have to go back to school to educate myself to be a veterinarian. I could form a sole proprietorship, go into sales, run an animal clinic, or do several other things. Thank you very much. I will explore these various opportunities."

I then suggested to Joe that a professional career specialist could help him define more exactly what his career calling would be and where he would best operate in his own niche. Through extensive psychological and vocational testing, Joe could arrive at a sense of direction in his life.

Remember, these three questions helped Joe, they have helped me, and hopefully they will help you if you are in a dilemma concerning your niche.

1. As a child what did you dream of becoming when you grew up?
2. Why did you want to become that of which you dreamed?
3. How did you arrive at your decision?

Once you explore your own answers to these questions, then a professional career counselor can help you get a more definite focus on your career niche. In fact, some career counselors specialize not only in career counseling but also in life planning; they can help you get a grip on your niche for your total life.

If you are properly capitalized, i.e., you have enough money to support your lifestyle for a few months up to a year, you will then be freer to pursue your niche. A person without a niche is like one trying to push a desk drawer closed when it is off its track. You can eventually force it closed but with much stress and resistance, and it never really fits. A person not in his niche is never truly comfortable and is constantly under stress — even though the individual may perform well in that position.

An individual in his niche is like a desk drawer on its track. It opens and closes smoothly and fits well. There is very little stress as it travels on its track because a major obstacle has been removed.

So get on track! Find your niche!

PERFECT YOUR SPECIAL, MARKETABLE SKILLS

Some of the things I like to do least are household chores, and Saturday morning is designated for these activities at my house. Often I sit on the family room couch staring at the carpet saying to myself: "I need to vacuum." Then my eyes wander around the room, and I think: "I need to dust." Sometimes in my procrastination I sit — waiting for "the spirit" to move me. However, there is a physical phenomenon I learned in physics class and that is: the spirit is lighter than the body, and it will never move me. I must move my spirit.

Many talented people with so much to offer are procrastinating, waiting to be moved to action by some outside unidentifiable source — little realizing that they are the only ones who can perfect their skills clusters. Vince Lombardi, coach of the Green Bay Packers, is credited with saying: "Practice doesn't make perfect. Perfect practice makes perfect." To perfect our skills then, we must practice those skills over and over perhaps for many years.

Olympic champion Jesse Owens had great natural ability as a runner, but he hewed, trained, and streamlined that ability until it became genius. All of us have talents, but there are so many people who are frustrated and disillusioned because they have never been able to apply their talents, thereby, never realizing their dreams.

Perfecting your natural skills clusters may not be easy. Many people work in a job all day and, even though tired, come home at night and work on a piece of art, practice a speech, or even study college courses. I am sure that every Olympic runner does not happily jump out of bed each day and eagerly anticipate twelve hours of conditioning for an event that may be eight years away. The key ingredient to perfection seems to be persistence, i.e., keeping on in spite of obstacles, failing, getting up, and trying again — and again — and again. Then one day that average person with persistence becomes a champion.

To perfect your skills, ask for feedback and assess that feedback, make necessary corrections in performance, and continue to practice the right things until you feel confident that you have a unique, quality product to offer.

CREATE A MARKET FOR YOUR SKILLS CLUSTERS

Not too long ago a friend from college days and I were talking. She said to me: "If I had known there were going to be only ten jobs in the city in my college major, I would have chosen some other specialty. Life is tough and rather insecure out here in the real world. It seems that there are 200 people competing for every position for which I apply."

She's right. In some cases, there is a narrow market for specific skills clusters. So, you either must be one of the very best in your field or find a unique, creative entrepreneurial outlet for your talents.

Another consideration is the ability to make a living from your talents. Many people find that monetary exchange for their talents will not support their lifestyle. Thus, they choose to have one vocation for financial support and an avocation for the self-expression of their talents.

However, the ideal situation results when, with painstaking research and patience and creativity, you find a primary career that allows you to do what you do best. You can accomplish this goal, but having talent is not enough. Unapplied talent is relatively useless. If you can create an outlet or market for your talents, you will rarely be without work no matter what economic conditions exist.

In 1932, Elmer Doolin noticed some corn chips at a borderline cafe in Texas. After negotiating with the Mexican chef, Mr. Doolin paid $100 for the recipe. After making several batches from the recipe, he named the product Fritos. This became the basis for the billion-dollar Frito-Lay company.

Continental Bakeries was suffering from the depressed economy of 1931. The plant manager, Jimmy Dewar, was hunting for a way to use the shortcake pans for something other than strawberry shortcakes because he could make strawberry shortcakes only during specific seasons of the year. Therefore, he put some dough into the pan and squirted a cream-type filling into the middle. This became what we know today as the Twinkie.

Fred Waring's relative could not eat solid food. Therefore, this band leader designed a device for liquefying vegetables in the 1930s. This device, of course, was the basis of the Waring Blender that we have today.[1]

Finding a creative use for a rather nondescript product escalated each of these people to the building of empires.

You can do it too. Through detailed, painstaking effort you can find a unique outlet for your skills clusters even if there is not a readily obvious one — such as accountant, teacher, doctor, or the like. Again, the road may not be easy to travel, and much persistence and patience may be required.

While in college, a friend's mother, Lucile Anderson, would often alleviate our discouragement by quoting: "Hitch your wagon to a star. Keep your seat, and there you are." To me this means that sometimes you have to be persistent in spite of obstacles even if you feel that you have exhausted all possibilities. After ten years of throwing away test batch after test batch of no-cholesterol, no-butterfat frozen dessert and after spending thousands of dollars,

David Mintz made it big. His company, Tofu, Time, Inc. created a frozen dessert based on soybean curd. His share of the company, which comes to over 51%, brought his worth to well over $10 million by 1984, and it has doubled since that time.[2]

Winston Churchill also failed at some things he tried. In fact, he failed the entrance exams to Sandhurst twice before he finally passed and was allowed to enter the school. Before Parlophone took the Beatles in 1962, their work had been rejected many times over. There are numerous stories about people who have made it big who had to try, and try, and try again before they ever got any attention. Persistence and tenacity are the basis for success for these people.

By believing in yourself and keeping on trying, eventually you will make it. Sometimes you have to apply your creativity. You must brainstorm, think of possibilities, and then go to work on those possibilities. For instance, if you enjoy archeology, anthropology, and ancient history, yet you have found entry into these fields very limited, you could organize a group of people, coordinate with a travel agent, and guide interested parties on a tour of Egypt or even a more rare, exotic place. You could charge a fee per person for your guide and lecture services. A whole entrepreneurial venture could be built around that concept. In fact, if your tours are interesting enough, it could be quite a lucrative venture for you.

Many good books explain how to conduct a self-directed job search and how to sell yourself to prospective employers. Professional career counselors can also offer guidance in this area.

You may already be in the job position where you can best excel. Congratulations! However, in the New Age, complacency will be dangerous. You will want to continue to look for ways to improve your performance and look for signals that your position is evolving. Nothing will be static in the New Age. Paraphrasing Will Rogers, "You may be on the right track, but if you don't keep on moving the train will hit you."

PACKAGE YOURSELF FOR IMPACT

Marketing tests indicate that many people cannot tell most soft drinks, coffee, and other types of drinks apart when the label is removed. One test shows that consumers believe that orange juice tastes better from cartons with a strong orange color than from cartons of a paler orange color.[3] Since the mid-1970s, producers of consumer items have learned that appealing packaging through label, design, logo, and color can be critical in

Declare Your Independence

determining which items people buy. Though no amount of packaging can make up for a poor quality product, it does have a great deal to do with initial selection.

In the New Age, when time is at a premium and change is rapid, you need to package yourself for greatest impact. You have from thirty seconds to four minutes to make a good first impression. Choose the image you wish to project—then acquire the clothes, behavior, and attitude that project that image. By consistently having that image, people will begin to think of you in that way. For example, if you wish to appear intelligent, you would dress in a dark, conservative professional suit; wear dark-rimmed glasses (whether or not you need them); cut your hair relatively short (for women who have long hair, wear it up); walk with an air of confidence; speak articulately; constantly acquire knowledge—through reading for a broad interest span; and practice good conversational skills.

You, to a great extent, control how people respond to you and what they think of you. In the New Age, which will have less structure and will promote individual differences rather than mass appeal, you have the freedom to envision how you want people to think of you.

I rarely cook. In fact, my husband hid my Christmas presents in the oven two years ago because he knew that was the only place I would never find them. I do know, however, that there are some basic requirements for a cake: flour, eggs, butter, salt, milk—to name a few. Eaten alone each ingredient would not taste very good, but if I mix them together in the proper proportions and bake them for the correct time period, the cake will be delicious.

The same principle is involved in personal and professional packaging. There are at least twelve identifiable ingredients of impact. You must decide how and in what combination you wish to use them. One entity alone will not necessarily cause great results, but used in your selected proportions, the results can be powerful.

Here are those ingredients and some suggestions about how you can use them for projection of impact.

1. Appearance

Recent UCLA studies indicate that over 50% of our communication is visual. You, then, set people up to respond to you mainly through your nonverbal communication, your physical appearance, and the clothes you wear. You then will select what clothes fit the image that you are trying to project, and then wear those clothes at the appropriate time. In addition, you will coordinate your hands, your arm movements, and all your nonverbal communication to project the communication that you want other people to receive from you. In addition, the practice of good physical fitness programs, good diet, exercise, and appropriate lifestyle can lead to a better appearance. Many delightful and informative books have been written about how to dress for a particular image, as well as proper diet and exercise. Your library will carry many of these books that will be helpful to you.

It is important to realize that appearance does not guarantee success. When you go into a bookstore to choose a book, you probably make an initial selection based on the cover. The title might intrigue you, the author's name might be one that you recognize, or you may even like the cover's color scheme. However, normally you do not buy the book until you have surveyed the contents and decided whether or not it is of enough value to you to pay the list price. The same dilemma occurs in your appearance, which merely helps people to make a positive selection. It does not guarantee your success. However, without a positive appearance, success is not as likely.

2. Personality

When I was a child, I believed that personality was inherited. I believed that you either had it or you didn't. Well, I was partially right. All of us are born with the dispensation toward a specific personality, but personality traits and characteristics can be learned. We tend to describe people as having a good personality, a sour personality, a sophisticated personality, a cultured personality, or a bad personality. But all of us do have personality. If you regard your personality as the sum total of all your traits, habits, and characteristics, you can work to develop one that is pleasant and that people enjoy having you project. In fact, it is very difficult to project an image of positive impact without good personality characteristics. So examine yourself. Do you have bad habits that you need to change? Do you need to improve your moods and attitudes? Do you have traits that you need to change? Are there any changes in your overall personality and behavior that you could make in order to improve your position in life? Once you work on the answers to some of these questions, then you will be able to have a more positive personality. Remember, personality traits, habits, and characteristics, although somewhat inborn, can be changed and controlled to a great extent by you.

3. Self-esteem

Positive self-esteem is a tremendous ingredient of impact. If you do not feel good about yourself, it is very difficult for others to feel good about you. You may feel that a projection of self-esteem comes from telling other people how good you are. Normally the opposite proves to be true. People who have self-confidence do not feel the need to tell people what they do well and to broadcast their accomplishments. They simply go about doing what they do best and know that other people will notice even if they do not comment on it.

You can project positive self-esteem by first knowing what you do best and knowing that you are the best at what you do. If you can instill this particular type of confidence in yourself without saying a word to other people, then that particular confidence will simply be an aura about you that other people will detect. Never allow yourself to be intimidated. Always remember that 99.9% of the people in the world have an inferiority complex—there is something about themselves that they would change if they could. Therefore, we all excel above others in something. Know that you do also. Like yourself. Know that you are constantly improving yourself. Know that God created you to be unique and different and that through positive self-esteem you can have tremendous impact.

4. Positive attitude

A positive attitude is a vitamin for your spirit. One of the major ways to impact other people is to maintain a positive attitude. People enjoy being around positive people. In fact, people are repelled by negative people. Just think of yourself. Do you really like being around people who are down all the time? When you have a friend who gets in a bad mood for six months, don't you get tired of it? When you pick up a newspaper, turn on the radio, or listen to the TV newscast, the most exciting news seems to be negative reporting. People are bombarded by negative messages day after day after day. So when you offer them the opportunity to be around a positive person, they will be drawn to you as if you were a magnet. However, positive attitude takes effort because the natural human default is to the negative.

Simply listen to typical coffee-break conversation. Normally that conversation leads to negative events, gossip about people, or derogatory remarks about the company. It really takes a supreme effort to keep the conversation positive. Positive conversation comes from the positive attitudes of its participants. Program yourself to be positive. Decide that you are going to be positive. Look for the silver lining in every cloud. One of my favorite Bible verses is Matthew 7:7 — "Ask and it shall be given you; seek and ye shall find; knock and it shall be opened unto you." I believe that a positive attitude will buffer you from many of the storms of life. I firmly believe that we can find something positive about every day of our lives, but we have to actively seek it — and by seeking, we will find it.

5. Goal-directed energy

Statistics indicate that only 2–3% of people in our nation set goals. Very few people are really headed anywhere. Goals are a part of the planning process that helps people to reach their dreams. Your energy can be put into behavior that will help you get what you want. It is important to set goals and then do your best to reach them. Goals have at least four parts to them. To have a goal it is important to

- set a target date to reach your goal
- know that the goal is achievable
- make certain your goal is worthwhile
- divide your goal into pieces so that you can reach your goal one step at a time.

Also, you may reserve the right to change directions. Very few people in their mid-thirties have the same goals for their lives that they had, for instance, at age seventeen. Either those goals of an early age have been reached or they no longer seem important. Reserve the right to change goals if they no longer interest you. There is a tremendous difference in changing goals because you wish, as opposed to quitting before you have reached your goal.

People of the greatest impact are headed somewhere. Once you set a goal and once you have begun to take steps toward reaching that goal, you will add to your impact upon others. People will enjoy being around you, and they will consider you a person who has a destination to his dreams.

6. Leadership skills

President Eisenhower illustrated his theory of leadership by putting a string on a table. He then pushed the string, and all it did was to curl up. It went nowhere. However, whenever he pulled the string, it followed him everywhere he wanted it to go. President Eisenhower believed that you lead not by pushing people, not by force and authoritarianism, but by pulling them along with you, for example, through friendship and through team building.

In the New Age, good leaders will have the ability to get people to do things because they wish, not because they must. There will be so much freedom of movement among employees and among the general population that authoritarianism will not work except in very specific circumstances. A leader who can facilitate development of the human resource area and who can coach people to achievement will be the one who will excel in the New Age.

You are a leader whether or not you are in a management position. Leadership occurs whenever you influence another individual, and all of us influence someone's life. It may be that you are a parent, a neighbor, someone's boss, someone's employee, someone's peer — whatever your role, you have the ability to exercise leadership over other people. Those who have good leadership skills and good team-building skills in the New Age will have greater impact than those who do not have these skills.

7. Conversational skills

The ability to converse with another person is of tantamount importance. Because we are living in an age demanding communication, you will be forced to communicate both technologically and person-to-person. The ability to carry on a conversation requires more than just talking and listening. Ask yourself the following questions:

1. Do you lose credibility by giving out information about which you are uninformed?
2. Do you practice active listening?
3. Do you monopolize the conversation?
4. Do you often finish other people's thoughts for them by interrupting?
5. Do you like to contradict the speaker?
6. Do you seem impatient while others are talking?
7. Do you often talk about yourself, your family or your own interests?
8. Do you like to gain attention by gossiping about others?
9. Do you go into too much detail?

10. Do you always tell the truth without exaggeration?
11. Do you continue to argue even if you realize that you are wrong?

If you answered all questions "No" except questions 2 and 10, pat yourself on the back. This is a good self-examination tool to determine your expertise in conversational skills.

8. Relational skills

Conversational skills are used in talking with someone on a one-on-one basis. In contrast, relational skills require the ability to establish a mutuality of interest between two parties. When you build a relationship, normally that mutuality extends over a long period of time. When you are able to relate to a person, you are able to talk with them and communicate with them on a basis past surface conversation. You are able to get them to express their feelings to you about their interests, about themselves personally, and about their business life.

A person who has a positive relationship with another individual carries a sense of confidentiality. When you are told something by another person, it is very important not to repeat that conversation to other people. In solid relationships, confidentiality is a form of respect.

Due to the nature of society in the New Age, relational skills are so important that they have been separated out as a strategy for success. You can read more about relational skills in Chapter 10.

9. Sense of humor

The ability to laugh at yourself with other people endears you to your friends and colleagues. If you cannot have a sense of humor about yourself and the mistakes you make, then it will be difficult to survive in the New Age. Life will proceed at a rapid pace, and much of your ability to cope with stress will depend on your sense of humor. Research indicates that people who enjoy life and are happy tend to have less sickness, absenteeism, and stress than people who take life very seriously and refuse to see life's lighter side.[4] Again, a sense of humor is a source of your personal impact. People enjoy being around enthusiastic individuals who enjoy life.

10. Broad interest span

Knowing a little about a lot of things can make you a very interesting person. This knowledge will be helpful in conversation

Declare Your Independence 83

and in establishing mutual relationships. Acquiring a broad interest span involves reading national newspapers and periodicals, listening to TV news reports, and reading about art, science, Broadway, movies, and other cultural events. By expanding your repertoire of interests, you can draw people out and have some knowledge of their interests. Remember, people's major interest is in themselves. If you can intelligently converse with them on their level about their interests, then you have planted the seed for good relationships.

11. Articulation skills

The first three letters of the word "articulation" spell the word "art." The ability to converse and to speak in public is an art form. Much emphasis is being placed on the ability to speak without interrupting your speech with such words as "uh" and "you know" or other habits that distract from your speaking ability. Most powerful individuals in the New Age will have articulation skills.

These particular skills can be developed through practice. One form of practice is to listen to yourself as you talk with other people. Try to catch yourself in habitual statements that might be displeasing to other people. You can also audiotape or videotape yourself, play it back, and analyze your own speaking techniques. Finally, you can take courses in speech or seminars on professional speaking and verbal communication. By joining such organizations as International Training and Communication and Toastmasters, you can be coached and have an ongoing educational program in speaking and leadership training.

12. Self-control

Most leaders practice self-control and have strict self-discipline. If you lose control of yourself in part of a situation, you normally become out-of-control of the entire situation. Self-discipline comes in the form of time management. You learn to say "Yes" to those things that will help you meet your goals and "No" to the things that are unimportant and that will distract from your pathway to success.

Self-control in your eating habits is also important. If you are overweight and unhealthy, you become a target for cardiovascular disease, cancer, and scores of other problems.

Discipline is also important in your emotions. Anger is one indication of an individual's being out-of-control. In fact, in a conflict situation, it is always helpful if you can control your anger. If you can keep this emotion under control, then you can dominate the situation in the end. One technique experts suggest we use to keep anger down is to picture the other person, the one who is angry, as a huge inflated balloon. As this person releases his anger, this balloon becomes deflated. Finally, the balloon will become flaccid, and we know a flaccid balloon has no power. Now you can control that balloon. A conflict situation is much like the situation with the balloon. The angry person will eventually deflate, and you can then win.

Conclusion

Your own personal packaging, then, will provide your distinct identity. In the next thirty years, unique identity will be a great tool to help you declare your independence.

PRACTICE CREATIVE SELF-PROMOTION

In the fast-paced New Age, you cannot wait to be discovered. You must find ways to bring favorable attention to yourself. Marketing yourself creates additional outlets for your talents and/or enhances your image in the eyes of your client base, i.e., such people as your employer, family, friends, and professional colleagues. In order to be a viable force in any group or relationship—especially in your company—it is important to have an ongoing program of self-promotion. You must be known for something. Prosperity in the New Age will fall to those with established, needed expertise. However, all the expertise in the world is no good unless people know about it. Here are twelve suggestions for self-promotion that people have found helpful.

1. Always perform with excellence.

Your best advertisement is a job well done. When you become known for the quality of your work, then you will be given more work to do. Nothing takes the place of excellence in the New Age.

Just last week I was standing in line for a movie. The fellow behind me was telling his companion about all the service problems that he had experienced the past week. It seems that he had leased a car instead of buying one simply for the ease of repairs. But every time he took the car in, they could not find the rattle that was aggravating him. He was even beginning to worry about the danger of driving the car, fearing there might be a problem with the brake system. He then took his personal computer in to be fixed, and they told him it would be at least three months before they could find the replacement part. I could sense his frustration because he had purchased the computer only two months previously. He then said that his video cassette recorder was only nine months old, and yet the heads needed to be realigned because the product was so sensitive.

His frustration was twofold. First, he had owned the products for only a short period of time, and they were already falling apart. But his major source of frustration was that he took the products in to be repaired multiple times before the service people could find the problems. He interpreted this as an indifferent attitude on the part of the service technicians. Whether this is true or whether the items are manufactured with such complexity that it is difficult to find the problem, people who do their job with excellence, who get it right the first time, and who deliver will be in great demand in the New Age. The public's frustration with poor service is reaching a boiling point.

2. Ask for assignments that showcase your strengths.

We don't always receive work assignments that display our strengths. Often we must do what it takes to get the job completed. But when there are slack times or you notice that a project is being delved out, be assertive — ask for those projects which will accentuate your strengths. When you can capitalize on your strengths and do those things that you do best, you then will be noticed for your prime performance.

3. Always keep an up-to-date resume.

Many people who have worked for corporations for a number of years either do not have a resume or have not updated a resume in years. It is helpful to keep a resume up-to-date with your latest accomplishments. With mergers and acquisitions at an all-time high, personnel records are probably being reviewed for new positions and shifting positions all the time. You never know when your personnel records are going before someone important to your career future. This technique is also good to keep you personally up-to-date on your own accomplishments. When you prepare a resume, you see how much you have accomplished in the past year or two. If you have no major accomplishments within the last twenty-four months for your resume, then perhaps you need to be adding to your repertoire of knowledge or seeking other assignments so that you can expand your base. In the New Age it is better to have multiple years of *experiences* than to have several years' *experience*.

4. Have on file a recent black and white publicity photo.

Approximately every three years have a professional photo made. This makes you feel professional and makes you feel good about yourself. Also, when you get publicity in the newspapers or in your company newsletter, it is impressive if you have a black and white photo available for them. Usually, the media prefers to take their own candid shot. However, when you have your own photograph, often the press will use it. A good professional picture taken by a professional photographer will highlight your best points and will make you look really good. That will then not only advertise you well, but will also escalate your self-esteem when you see yourself in print.

5. Secure an agent.

Corporations and people in business for themselves often hire a public relations firm to help them get attention. Entertainers employ agents to find clients and to set up performances as well as to negotiate their contracts.

You may feel that it is senseless to hire an agent if you are a corporate employee. But think of it this way: you probably have one already in place in the organization. You may have never thought about your supporters in this way. Each of us in the organization, if we do a good job and if we have impact, has someone who admires our work a great deal. When you volunteer for a project or when you are trying to get a promotion, ask this person to help you. Ask him or her to write letters of recommendation.

One of the most compelling questions that you can ask an individual who admires you is: "Will you help me?" People enjoy helping individuals they admire. They will enjoy helping you more if you reward them by saying "thank you" or by taking them to dinner. You don't have to offer monetary rewards, in fact that may not even be in good taste, but give them special attention. Never fail to say "thank you" when someone helps you. You do have an agent. The challenge is to find and use this agent in a positive way for success. Your agent will respect you for it.

6. Acquire letters of commendation.

When you have done a good job on a project, have saved the company money, or have had a new idea that is workable, it is always helpful if someone will write a letter to upper management about you. If the project was outside your company, get someone to write a letter of commendation to your manager. Most people never think to do this. In a rushed world which will increase in speed in the New Age, it is going to be more difficult to get people to commend us in letter form.

Personally, I do not like to ask for letters of commendation. Some people have no problem with asking for these letters. If you feel comfortable asking someone to write a letter about you, then do it. However, if you feel uncomfortable asking someone to compliment you, then you can write a letter thanking them for the opportunity of working with them. Often those people will answer your letter with those compliments you deserve. You, then, can copy this letter to your management. Or you might have someone else ask for the letter for you. You might have your admirer or agent have lunch with them, if there is a mutual relationship between your agent and the other person, and have your agent suggest that a letter be written about you. Third-party requests are always more effective than your asking for yourself.

7. Publish articles.

If you want favorable attention, publishing articles in your area of expertise makes you an immediate expert. People who publish articles are given eminence and importance by their readers. Of course, it is understood that the article should be accurate and up-to-date. Many magazines in your special field are looking for articles that are creative, new, and that take a different angle from what they have been publishing before.

Fresh new material is difficult to find in the publishing world, so magazines are always looking for someone like you to give them a publishable article. There are so many different competitive media out today that it should not be difficult to find someone to publish your material. The real value in publishing articles is in acquiring reprints. After your article is published, order several reprints so that you can put one in your personnel file and use others for your own publicity. Publishing is one avenue to immediate celebrity status in your field.

8. Feature yourself (or get featured) on TV and radio.

This may seem a little farfetched to you. Perhaps you do not feel that you have done anything of significance that the radio and TV media would favor. However, radio and television talk shows are always looking for interesting people. They must have from one to five people every day on their talk shows. Perhaps you will not immediately climb to national status, but there are plenty of local stations that would be happy to have you, especially if you are a published person. You can get a list of the radio stations and the talk show hosts or public relations people at the stations. Call them yourself and tell them what you are doing that might be of interest.

An even better way is to have an objective third party call or write the stations. A third party can always compliment you more highly and have it seem more sincere than you can compliment yourself. Your discomfort in complimenting yourself normally comes through. It is a good idea to have your resume, your professional photograph, and article reprints available so that the radio and television hosts can review these in making a decision to have you on the show. If possible, always talk about your company and its accomplishments—use its name as well as yours. This is good free publicity not only for you but also for your company.

9. Write a book.

Very few people read books. Approximately 5% of Americans read a book every year. However, Americans buy books prolifically. They scan the books for interesting information, but rarely read them from cover to cover. If you have a topic of interest that is new, refreshing, and contemporary, type a manuscript and submit it to several publishers. Perhaps one of them will pick up on your idea and publish your book.

To have a book published will increase your stature not only in your company but also in your own eyes. In looking for other positions outside your company or for transferring from one position to another within your company, the fact that you have written a book within your area of expertise—especially if your expertise is being used in your company—will help you tremendously.

Getting a book published is a landmark in a person's life. It shows that you can complete a project, that you can organize your thoughts, and that someone else is willing to buy your ideas.

10. Speak on your topic.

Organizations, both professional and social, are always looking for speakers for their meetings. Many organizations do not pay professional speakers. These organizations are a wonderful place to showcase your talents. Simply compile your resume, your

Declare Your Independence

professional photograph, reprints, and any other information about yourself, and enclose these with a letter (preferably written by someone else) suggesting that you speak at one of their meetings. Send this letter and information to program chairpeople or any person of influence in the club who knows you and can help you get on the program.

Another self-promotion speaking technique is to teach classes. Often your own organization has classes in your area of expertise. Teaching not only helps you to keep up with state-of-the-art programs in your area, but it also helps to keep other people up-to-date on new information. Local junior colleges, churches, parishes, and synagogues all have programs in various areas. So the teaching of classes is one possible avenue that can promote your talents to other people.

11. Become an agent for your company.

Carry the banner for someone else. If there is someone in the company that you feel is doing a good job and you are in a position of recommendation, then recommend that person for a new position or one that will use his or her talents better. Be an agent for someone else. If there is an opportunity to get publicity for someone else or to get publicity for your company, then let that other person have the attention. By helping other people, you also help yourself. Eventually, that help will be reciprocated.

12. Involve yourself in outside activities.

Social, professional, and charitable organizations all need you. You can make tremendous contributions to these organizations with your time and your service. There are numerous organizations that are advertising for help today. Often these organizations allow you to showcase your major talents and capitalize on your major strengths when your company is not in a position to do so. In addition, you meet other people and form strong friendships in these organizations while feeling good about yourself.

Often what you are doing for a volunteer activity is the very thing that will escalate you into becoming more what you want to be. Your work in the community and outside your own company very often will get you more promotion and publicity than those things which you are doing internal to your company.

A good balance, of course, is necessary. Some people get so involved in their outside activities that it is detrimental to their work life. Always keep in mind that your vocation comes first for your energy and for your efforts. The source from which you earn a living is of primary importance to you. However, it is helpful if you can hold offices in other organizations and do a good job. One caveat, however, is: never assume a responsibility that you cannot handle. It is much worse to have a position of responsibility and not do a good job than to decline that position of responsibility. If you know you are going to be too busy to handle a job or if you have taken a responsibility and have suddenly become too busy to handle it, then resign. *Never do a bad job.* That reputation travels much faster than having done a good job.

Remember, in the New Age you cannot sit back and wait to be discovered. You must promote yourself tactfully but assuredly. Self-promotion is one of the greatest investments that you can make in yourself, your career, and your future.

BE A TEAM PLAYER

Much has been written about team building and coaching, but little has been mentioned about team participation. Though you declare your independence, it is important that you have the ability to be a team player — to make contributions to something bigger than yourself — your company, family, religious affiliation, professional groups, nation, and social circles. When you declare your independence, i.e., you become a free agent, you have security in knowing that there are probably several teams on which you can play — not just one. But while you are playing for a selected team, give the position your best. You must have total commitment to the team and do your part in contributing to its success. The idea is to play your heart out for the team but to always have contingency plans in mind in case you decide to leave the team — or the team decides to leave you. Often severance is beyond the control of both team and player.

Whether people recognize it or not, all of us play on a team. We contribute to some group relationship. Very few people are so isolated and self-sufficient that they can escape participation of some sort. Remember, being a team player is an avenue of service. Many executives have found that the secret of leadership comes through serving.

In order to prosper in the New Age, corporate leaders will serve subordinates, and companies will serve their customers. Here are eight rules for becoming a good team player.

1. Select a position that maximizes your talents.

When you are given the opportunity, always ask for a position in your corporation or ask for responsibility in an organization or on a committee that will showcase your talents. When you are in a position that maximizes your talents, then you can give that position your best. Sometimes you may select a position that will challenge your talents. Perhaps these talents have never been used to that extent before. For instance, when I was a child, I decided I wanted to be a pitcher on the girls' softball team. When I tried out for pitcher that summer, I couldn't even get the ball near the batter. However, I did have the talent to get the ball from the pitcher's box over the plate even though there was a variance of several feet. What I needed was more control to perfect the pitching skill. My challenge for the summer was to practice pitching so that the next year, when I went out for pitcher in the tryouts, I would be ready.

2. Practice, practice, practice.

All that summer I practiced every day. My mother, my peers, my father—everybody concerned—would assume the position of catcher. Every day I practiced getting the ball over the plate and into the catcher's mitt. I practiced for hours. Thank God for the patience of my family and friends!

The next summer when I went out for pitcher, I qualified. The basic skills were there all the time. They merely had to be tailored, practiced, and developed.

Often, when we play a position at work, in our family, or in other areas of our lives, the skills for that role are not totally developed. They must be tailored into genius. They must be practiced into perfection. If you want something badly enough and are willing to work for it, then you can develop your talents into those that are the best in your business.

3. Support the other players on the team.

A good team player is always too big to belittle. A good team player never gossips to other members about a specific team member. That comrade is always supportive of the team. A good team member realizes that he or she alone cannot produce a winning team. A coach alone cannot produce a winning team. It takes all players executing their various responsibilities to cause a team to win.

At your work and in the various roles you play, the same principle exists. You in cooperation with other people become more powerful than you can be by yourself. And though you have mentally and financially declared your independence, you will by choice have a team and be a member of a team that will make you stronger than you are by yourself. When you seek to destroy other team members or embarrass the team through negative behavior, then you defeat only yourself. Your ultimate strength comes from being a part of something that has more strength than you can provide on your own.

4. Respect the coach's position.

Not all people like their coach. Most players, however, respect the coach's position. At work your boss might not be the individual that you would choose to be your friend. The ideal situation occurs when your boss is your friend. But on rare occasions your boss or coach does not measure up to the qualities you like in a person. However, the position of that person, normally your superior, is to be respected. Someone obviously felt that your superior could do the job or that superior would not have been appointed to that position. You must have faith that if this person is incompetent, then he eventually will be removed.

This situation can sometimes be very uncomfortable, and often you have to remove yourself from the situation. However, it is normally better for you to seek another team or another position rather than to try to go around your superior or make your superior look bad. So, respect the coach's position, and do what you have to do to continue making yourself look good without embarrassing your superior.

5. Be humble in spite of your success.

A mother commented to me that she wished her daughter would come home from college just one time and be interested in something other than herself. The mother went on to say that her daughter is always bragging on her own accomplishments and is always patting herself on the back for her good grades. The mother feels that perhaps she has unintentionally created a monster in her daughter.

The daughter probably feels her mother wants to hear these things, but even our parents grow tired of hearing us compliment ourselves. They like to talk about themselves, too. Remember, a person's favorite subject is self. Even when you are close to someone — your spouse, your best friend, your sister or brother — it is not in good taste to compliment yourself. Compliment the other person; build them up in your eyes. Chances are that if you have accomplished something of significance, they know about it. When you are humble and say nothing about it at work or in your private life, that endears you to your colleagues, your peers, and your family more than if you constantly praise yourself. There is definitely a place for more humility on every team. A humble person is a confident person.

6. Be helpful to other team members.

In order not to alienate other team players or cause internal cliques to form, share the workload. Cover for your team members if they are not feeling well or if there are problems in their personal lives. Normally when we treat people as we would like to be treated, they reciprocate when we have specific needs.

On consulting assignments, when I am interviewing employees concerning job responsibilities, I often hear: "That's not my job." Sometimes you will be called on to do work that is not your job. A good team member feels that the real job is to do whatever it takes to cause the team to look good, forgets about being tired, and works extra time to help other team members. In addition, good team members do not criticize others for their lack of effort. They do their best to promote a win for the team as a whole.

7. Service the team members' personal needs.

Whether or not it is pleasant for us, we work with a whole person. Our team members all have personal problems and needs that sometimes are so overbearing that they cannot separate them from their work. A show of concern is often just what the other person needs. You need to be careful not to show so much sympathy that the other person uses you as a listener to the point that neither one of you gets any work done. However, caring for other persons and pitching in to help when they are not feeling well normally will deepen a relationship with your team members.

We all have personal needs. Some of these needs are more prevalent at one time than another. In the New Age, when there is so much automation and people are going at breakneck speeds to meet deadlines and goals, the individual who takes time to really care for someone else will be a valuable, viable part of the team.

8. Keep calm under pressure.

Most great football teams report having been in tight spots down to the last few seconds of the game. By keeping cool heads and continuing to play the game, many teams have won in the last second. The game is not over until the whistle blows.

Sometimes when we allow stress to overcome us or our emotions to explode, we lose control of the situation. When we lose our calm, very often that is the key to losing the game. The ability to handle stress is going to be one of the primary issues of the future. I can't say enough about prioritizing your time, learning self-talk procedures to control your emotions, and getting yourself together so that under pressure you will be able to respond. In the New Age, we sometimes feel that we are playing out life in a pressure cooker. However, if you can learn to cope with the pressures surrounding you and perform with excellence even under these conditions, then you will be a star player on the team.

Harry Truman once said, "If you don't like the heat in the kitchen, get out." That was a Second Wave comment because in the New Age if you don't like the heat in the kitchen, there won't be any other place to go. Your only option is to learn control techniques, i.e., keep calm under pressure.

Conclusion

Although it may take concentrated effort, it is possible to *declare your independence*. When you do, you will enhance your self-confidence and increase your contributions to the world about you.

Summary:
1. Americans are beginning to feel victimized by rapid corporate and family changes and are puzzled about how to resolve their attitude to accept a lifestyle much different from that of which they had dreamed.
2. Dependency, both psychological and financial, can be devastating. The first step toward power positioning is to declare your independence.
3. You can declare your independence by going into business with yourself, i.e., forming an indipreneurship.
4. The same principles that make a business successful can be used to make your indipreneurship successful. There are seven steps for success in declaring your independence.
    - Create a strong investment and savings program.
    - Find your niche.
    - Perfect your special, unique, marketable skills clusters.
    - Create a market for your skills clusters.
    - Package yourself for personal impact.
    - Practice creative self-promotion techniques.
    - Be a team player.

Chapter 7

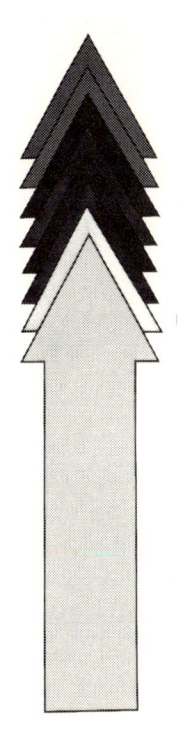

Anticipate Tomorrow's Business World

> *Nothing is more terrible than activity without insight.*
> —Thomas Carlyle

The future business world holds the potential for great excitement and promise. In an era of short shelf-life and targeted prosperity, our very career survival, however, depends on our ability to anticipate that world and to be prepared ahead of time for shakeups in the work place and shakedowns in the work force.

In the New Age, adaptation to change is not enough. You must anticipate it. Adapting occurs after the fact; in the New Age "after" is too late. You must be in place before change in order to prosper: i.e., *pioneer your position*. Whether you are an employee or an independent business owner, tomorrow's business world will be a viable part of your future. Key strategies, then, to prepare for your career future are: anticipate, assimilate, innovate, and educate. Based on our research, here are some of our ideas about the future of business in America.

Since projections can often become perilous and fail to live up to expectations, we need to be cautious of overly optimistic prophecies of the future. For example, just over thirty years ago, in 1955, several prominent thinkers, business people, and government officials prophesied into the 1980s. Their hopes and ideas were published in *Fortune* and later appeared in a book entitled *The Fabulous Future, America in 1980*. They predicted that by 1980

- atomic batteries would be practical
- solar energy would be developed
- helicopters would be in prevalent use
- the 1980s would be an era of leisure and abundance
- energy would be cost-free
- average American family expendable income would be approximately $8,000 per year
- new avenues would open for solid-state electronics
- nuclear fission would not suffice for energy needs, and
- solar, rather than nuclear, energy would have more lasting benefits.[1]

As you can see, most of the crystal ball predictions have not yet come to pass. Only a few have been introduced into our lives. Historically, although innovation and change are rapid, they rarely occur with the speed or even in the same manner as predicted. Unforeseen barriers usually slow down growth. Also, the human factor enters the picture. With consideration for the preservation of jobs and "wants" of a particular society, technology can present us with enormous potential, but it continues to take people to make things happen. So for the sake of prediction, let's list some needs of tomorrow's workers and business executives.

- To profit under heavy competition
- To increase productivity in the manufacturing and service sectors
- To provide retraining for people in displaced jobs
- To train people for new career positions
- To make work enjoyable
- To manage a diverse group of employees with an individual participative rather than a mass authoritative approach
- To create less restricted schedules for the work force
- To allow more freedom and creativity on the job
- To treat the employee as a whole "person" rather than as a worker
- To increase knowledge of and use of automation

With these needs in mind, you have probably already surmised that tomorrow's business world will be as different as today's era is from that of the Pony Express. Though we must merely extrapolate from today, we will hopefully make fewer perilous predictions than our historical predecessors.

GENERAL CHARACTERISTICS OF TOMORROW'S BUSINESS WORLD

Influenced by international joint ventures and immigration (which will account for two-thirds of America's population growth by the year 2000),[2] American companies will become a convolution of cultures and value systems. Foreign companies located in America will employ Americans and U. S. companies will employ non-native-born Americans. In fact, all states will be competing for foreign industry to boost their respective economies. For the six months ending September 30, 1985, $35.7 million flowed out of Japan alone into United States investments, loans, and the purchase of U. S. Savings Bonds. Offshore investors spent in excess of $10 billion on U. S. properties in 1985, and that figure is expected to grow each year for the next several years.[3] American business will have dominant foreign influence.

For the next fifteen years, the career marketplace in traditional fields will be highly competitive as the transition takes place to more automation. For people in the work force born before 1955, many were not exposed to the computer in school, and corporate culture shock will be prevalent among those workers. People thirty years of age and younger will be better able to adapt to a changing work world because of more exposure to automation in schools as they grew up. Foreign and domestic competition, increased integration of educated people (many of whom will hold graduate degrees), and computerization of the work place will cause much competition for such positions as Second Wave manufacturing, assembly line, clerical, shop, and administrative assistant jobs.

In order to respond to market demands, business life will be fast paced and ever changing. Those people who have not learned to cope with stress will find difficulty adjusting to the rapid pace of the business world. In fact, consultants, physicians, and trainers in the stress management business should find their accounts booming, thereby providing job security for many years hence for these professionals.

Productivity, especially in the service sector, will be a key issue. Robert Half International surveyed 312 corporations from coast to coast and found that the average employee wastes four hours and eighteen minutes per week. The study also concluded that service industry workers, because of a more freely structured environment, wasted 30% more time than manufacturing workers.[4] Extrapolated into the future, we project that more time will be wasted and new productivity measures must be designed in order to increase quality and service in the work place. Because service is not necessarily measured in quantitative output per person-hour but is measured in quality, the development of new productivity measures will then bring about new reward and incentive systems.

Corporations will pare as much overhead as possible (especially in health care) without cutting too heavily into the benefits of full-time employees. Goodyear Tire and Rubber Company of Lawton, Oklahoma, has already opened its own employee medical center. It is such a financial success that the company is contemplating duplicating the concept in other locations. To cut its health care costs, Southern California Edison pays medical claims directly from employee premiums. In addition, the company owns its own pharmacy and has nine medical clinics. Preferred Provider Organizations (PPOs) are being used by smaller companies that cannot afford their own in-house health care facilities. These PPOs rate hospitals and doctors and negotiate discounted fee schedules in return for prompt payment and a large volume of business.[5]

Because of the great need for specialized knowledge and cost cutting, many corporations will make use of subcontractors and outside consultants—especially if these services are not required on a regular basis. This will cut down on office overhead and on the need to furnish employee benefits to so many people. In addition, corporations will be able to avail themselves of state-of-the-art, broader scope, up-to-date information from consultants, whose sole job is to stay informed about their field of expertise.

Smaller businesses will find their specialized niche for strength and fast growth. Most jobs will be created in these smaller entrepreneurial companies while the more mature, older, slower growth companies will diversify for added growth and strength. Philip Morris's $5.6 billion acquisition of General Foods and R. J. Reynolds's buyout of Nabisco diversified these tobacco companies into the consumer products areas. The Washington-based law firm, Arnold and Porter, operates subsidiaries specializing in real estate and financial services. A Phoenix law firm, Van O'Steen and Partners, has expanded into advertising and marketing. Large accounting firms are moving into human resource consulting and into computer training.[6] Professional services, especially those that are large enough, will take the holistic approach to the customer. Survival will be more difficult for small specialized professional services in the future, and many will find themselves targets for buyouts by the larger organizations.

REDEFINITION OF THE WORK PLACE

Physical work place layout will be transformed by high technology. The office will become more and more paperless, thus eliminating the need for massive warehousing of files while computers will provide storage for millions of characters of data. Electronic work stations housed in giant acoustical rooms or in private cubicles will substitute for many of the walled offices of today. According to SRI International, by 1990 there will be more than 17.5 million of these electronic work stations in the United States alone. Noise level of future computers and printers will be much less than those of today. Many of the office machines of the future will be voice-activated — typewriters, cathode ray tubes, telephones, and the like — and will eliminate the magnitude of manual labor involved in inputting, processing, and storing information. By the mid-1990s, other storage devices, such as video discs, will have the capacity to store millions of pages of data on one record-size plate.[7]

Since more safety, productivity, and honesty will be corporate goals, microcomputers which whisper such messages as "safety first" and "be honest, don't steal" in a deep resonant voice will be implemented. In fact, in excess of 100 companies are already applying this technique today. This Threshold Messaging System patented by Proactive Systems Incorporated broadcasts messages up to 600 times per hour just at the threshold of conscious hearing.[8] Other such devices will be developed to suggest better time management, faster production, and quality service as we learn more about messaging and threshold suggestion techniques. That will be a painless way to increase employee productivity, change employee culture, or alter dress code without management intervention and employee counseling.

Security guards will be replaced by robots that will have the ability to prevent sabotage or destruction by an intruder with some kind of nonlethal weapon such as tear gas. Since most security guards' jobs tend to be monotonous, boring, and physically demanding, robots will alleviate many of these factors. These automated devices will detect smoke, movement around the periphery, and rapid temperature changes. The robot would be equipped with a motion sensor and a closed circuit television system. The robot then will alert a central control station, and that control station can take action via a televised picture transmitted by the robot. Each robotic security system will be tailored to a particular industry and physical layout. Although the initial design will be very expensive, it is projected that the company will reach a break-even point in approximately one year by having a robot system as opposed to a system physically guarded by humans for three shifts per day. Two companies already envisioning the use of robots and producing this type of system are Advance Security and 21st Century Robotics.[9]

Much as the computer industry was a fledgling in the late 1950s and early 1960s, the robot industry will be the new babe of the 1990s. Manufacturers are already retooling for installation of robots to do many of the jobs now held by assembly-line workers. It is projected that 800,000 robots will be in the United States by 2001. According to a Techtran Corporation forecast, the number of robots installed within the next five years will quadruple to 50,000 from 14,400 today.[10]

Due to the capability of technological interconnection, remote work sites will be scattered worldwide. With computer terminals, personal computer networks, and cellular telephones, work sites can be virtually anywhere including in one's automobile. This interconnection capability will give rise to telecommuting, i.e., working from home or some other remote site. This will cut down on needed office space and will eliminate daily long distance drives into the office.

Research already shows that disciplined employees who work at home put in more hours on the job, have less absenteeism, and greater longevity with the company. Take-charge, self-starting employees have already proven productivity increase without close supervision. Managers have also indicated satisfaction with this situation. Possibly 25–35% of the work force will be telecommuters by the year 2000.[11]

Technological interconnectedness has far-reaching implications. It means decentralization of urban areas, more remote suburban or rural living, less crowding of highways, less automobile fuel consumption, and less wasted commuter time.

In some ways, automation will complicate the work place. New technology will make machines harder to use in a few cases. For example, one instruction book today on how to make the personal computer simple is in excess of 400 pages in length. The average non-computer-oriented individual finds it very difficult to interpret this "easy to read" book. For those employees without a technical mind-set or who suffer "technofright," the computer will be temporarily malproductive.[12] Until people understand the computer's usefulness as a tool rather than a job threat, automation will be slower and more stressful. It will not totally revolutionize the office environment as rapidly as computer vendors would like to see occur.

In the transition to new systems, new applications, and prolific use of robots, the work place will be very frustrating to many employees. The users will suffer through many system "bugs" and robot malfunctions. With the advent of so many novel technologies simultaneously, there will be much confusion and frustration. If organizations attempt too much technical innovation without proper system planning, the work place will resemble bedlam. One of the two inventors of the microchip in 1959 (Robert N. Noyce, vice-chairman of Intel Corporation) feels that the U. S. work place is a quarter of a century away from having the ultimate user-friendly computer that will be manipulated comfortably and extensively by an affable user. Until then, the revolution will be merely a progressive evolution.

THE SHIFTING WORK FORCE

By the year 2000, 85% of U. S. workers will be in the trade and service work sector. In 1984, only 52% of civilians were employed in these two industries. According to the U. S. Bureau of Labor Statistics, 90% of new jobs to be created during the next ten years will include services; and that will encompass everything from cutting hair and selling insurance policies to performing liver and heart transplants. Workers collectively will be different in composition fifteen years hence from what they are today in terms of skills, education level, age, rewards expected, and independence demanded. The new service and information work place will lend itself well to a new and creative work force.[13]

Cognitive and substantive workers

Workers will easily divide into two categories according to dominant function used to execute tasks: (1) cognitive and (2) substantive. All labor will be skilled. If individuals do not apply a useful skill, they will be replaced by automation. Workers with cognitive skills will work mostly with information—inputting, storing, retrieving, manipulating, extrapolating, synthesizing, projecting, and transmitting. This group will be divided into four types: UMPs, LMPs, DMPs, and GSPs.

UMPs or Upwardly Mobile Professionals will be those who seek leadership positions within the organization. Generally, they will have at least one college degree and many will hold graduate and postgraduate degrees. Their basic skills will be in managing a diverse employee population, generating profits, and relationship building both internal and external to the organization. Many UMPs will aspire to these peak ranks, but few will obtain them because mid-level management will continue to decrease in number of positions available and fewer top-level positions will be vacated. For those entrepreneur-spirited hopefuls, the one best way to make it to the top will be to start and build their own company—and many will do just that as more workers become dissatisfied with their jobs.

A Chicago industrial psychology firm, Stanard and Associates, surveyed 4,000 workers in 1976–1980 then surveyed a comparable number of workers from 1981 to 1984. They found a steady decrease in employee satisfaction in almost every category surveyed except for employee benefits. Morale is dropping in the areas of pay, job security, perceived effectiveness of administration, confidence in management, corporate communication with employees, and women's perception of their satisfaction on the job. This trend will continue during the next five years as the work place continues to be in transition toward new employee cultures.[14]

LMPs or Laterally Mobile Professionals will be those workers who have specific skills clusters which they wish to hone. This group includes specialists in particular fields—engineers, doctors, lawyers, accountants, computer programmers, pharmacists, nurses, and teachers, just to name a few. Their functions will change as their professions evolve, but they will choose to spend their careers connected in some way to a particular field or specialty. The major portion of the labor force will function as LMPs. These people do not aspire to high positions of leadership because their career rewards come from their field of specialty and in being the best that they can be in that particular position.

DMPs or Downwardly Mobile Professionals will be the "has beens," i.e., the elite professionals of today who refuse to acknowledge the need for update and change. Their slogan will be, "We have always done it this way" and "if it ain't broke, don't fix it." These people will be candidates for display in the Smithsonian, and we will visit them on our future trips to Washington. Typically, these people were born earlier than 1955 and have performed adequately for years. As automation decreases the need for mid-management, some people will be vulnerable; for example, financial analysts, production and inventory controllers, researchers, executive assistants, and anyone who thinks traditionally or refuses to learn how to apply automation as a tool to enhance his or her position.[15]

GSPs or Generalized Skills Professionals are those workers whose skills clusters can transfer across positions. However, these people are not UMPs nor are they specialists as are the LMPs. Supervisors, secretaries, clerks, and salespeople fall into this category. Their skills will be useful in many lines of endeavor.

The second broad category — substantive skills workers — will be used predominantly in tasks that require physical labor. These individuals will also need to be aware of computers and automation but will not be directly linked to information creation and dissemination as a profession. Automation will be used merely to make their jobs easier and more productive. Among those workers in this category are truck drivers, mechanics, repair technicians, janitors, carpenters, plumbers, and electricians. New York's J. Walter Thompson ad agency identified this group as elite workers, many of whom earn greater than $30,000 per year even without college educations.[16]

Educated labor

Education and training will be required for jobs in the future. The work force is already more educated now than at any other time in American history. In 1985, a quarter of the U. S. population had some college education (up to a degree or more). In 1995, it is estimated that 50% of the U. S. population will have some college education (up to a degree or more).[17]

Colleges will be forced to restructure teaching techniques and curriculum development. Outside fields of specialization, more emphasis will be placed on identification and development of skills clusters as opposed to rote memorization due to the rapidity of information becoming obsolete. Rather than memorizing information, students will be taught how to research information and how to synthesize it into useful application. Much instruction will be via computer-managed instruction devices and simulation techniques. Students will be taught *how* to think rather than *what* to think. Dean Raymond E. Miles of the School of Business Administration, the University of California at Berkeley, has proposed a new system of business education. In his article, "The Future of Business Education," released in the spring 1985 issue of *The*

California Management Review, Dean Miles states that business schools of the 1990s must have a multilevel approach to educate three types of business majors: specialists, generalists, and teachers. He believes that the multitiered curriculum could be composed of:

- A general business major or minor that will involve no more than six to eight semester courses in business and will be built on a strong general business and organizational program but will not have a functional specialization at that particular level.
- Master's degree program which will concentrate on one of several business specialties and will be five years in length. At this point, special skills clusters and economic and business issues will be solidified, and an internship would take place between the fourth and fifth years of education. Dean Miles believes that CPA firms and other specialized business institutions would be interested in this phase. He also feels that four years in the accounting field is not long enough to teach the concentration.
- A two-year general management M.B.A. program that would be offered to experienced managers in lieu of the five-year master's program. This program would be designed for the group we have labeled UMPs.
- A part-time Executive D.B.A. (Doctor of Business Administration) which would be designed for specialists who want to concentrate their skills clusters. This program would reenforce the skills of the LMPs. High-level staff executives as well as consultants would be interested in this approach.
- A Ph.D. that would exist for the training of a teaching faculty. This course of study would be academic as opposed to application oriented.
- Continuing management education which would be creative as opposed to structured, designed to broaden the horizons of management, and continue throughout the life span of the management career.[18]

Graying employees

The work force will be middle-aged by 2010; 50% of the population will be over forty. By the year 2000, the median age of the population is expected to exceed age thirty-six. Due to the decline in birth rates after 1965, there was a "baby bust." These people are now beginning to enter the work force as the maturing baby boomers move up and through the ranks. By 2000, the initial group of baby boomers will reach the early retirement age of fifty-five and will begin leaving the work force. It is estimated that 80% of people fifty-five and over will be out of the work force by that time.[19] And eventually, by 2020, there will be a greatly reduced number of employees in organizations. If the evolution of automation keeps pace with the decline in work force, then natural attrition will help resolve the challenge of job displacement. The baby bust generation will then have less stress and higher income per capita than their parents.

There will be a growing respect for older workers, and there will be less emphasis on youth (although there will be an eternal interest in youthfulness). Even as early as 1988, large corporations could feel an employee shortage, thereby forcing them to look to alternative sources of labor. Retirees will be a likely source, and most will be employed part time in non-managerial positions. Travelers Insurance Company and Texas Refinery are among companies finding that older workers can increase profit. By 1990, approximately 30% of the labor force will be forty-five or older. However, during the years approaching the twenty-first century, older workers will continue to feel pushed aside for younger workers and for automation.[20] Executives and specialists of Second Wave industries may be laid off in middle age and find that locating a similar position may be difficult or impossible.[21]

For all the work force shakeup in coming years, it is a "given" that companies will employ older people; first out of necessity, then they will eventually discover that age and career obsolescence do not necessarily go hand in hand. The older worker will gain new respect in the work place.

Employee-driven

In the industrial economy of the Second Wave, companies were largely leader-driven, but in an information economy the people *are* the company. Without human capital, service and information organizations cannot function. The best investment that companies will make in the next fifteen years will be in their people. Rather than treat people as disposable commodities, successful companies will treat their people as an economic necessity. Thus most companies will realize that their organizations are employee-driven. Some ways employees will drive corporations are:

- participative decision making and ownership
- flexible lifestyle scheduling

- cafeteria-style benefits programs
- performance-based reward systems, and
- increased company liability for employees.

There will be more lateral training in various departments to acquaint employees with the whole organization. Understanding other employees' roles will foster less conflict and better interpretation of other people's responsibilities. More trust will be built between employee and company, and this trust will be earned by all parties.[22] Leaders will ask employees to suggest changes and ideas for better company performance. This input will then be justly rewarded. Ownership in the corporation will be promoted. Expanded use of stock ownership plans, profit-sharing, and other creative employee benefit programs will allow employees to feel the pride of proprietorship. Employees will then know that their performance affects their own pocketbooks. Good leaders of such diverse and employee-driven companies will be rare and will come at a premium. Relationship management will be the evolving emphasis over the next fifteen years.

Due to varied lifestyles, employee work time will have a less rigid structure. The following statistics indicate flexibility in the work place.

- Less than 60% of households contain married couples.
- Greater than 40% of the current work force are two-income families.
- Sixty percent of all mothers work outside the home.
- Greater than a quarter of all the labor force are single.[23]

And these numbers will grow in their respective categories as we approach the year 2000.

Work options will become increasingly available for the varied lifestyles:

- *Job sharing*, where two or more people share the same job function, will be prevalent. This arrangement will be particularly inviting to mothers and fathers of small children as well as to retirees.
- *Voluntary reduced work time* will be available for individuals who are not wanting to work full time for any reason, be it a young mother, a retiree, or an individual who seems to have ample income and wants to have a reduced workload throughout life. Voluntary reduced work time entails also a voluntary reduced income. Part time, as we know it today constituting work for less than thirty-two hours per week in 1985, will probably be less than twenty-five hours a week in

the year 2000 because full-time workers may not work more than thirty-two to thirty-six hours per week by the year 2000.
- *Flextime* allows employees to come and go within a set time schedule. For instance, workers may work nine to five, seven to three, or ten to six. In order to keep the job continuity, employees will overlap times. While one person comes in ten to six, another may work seven to three to see that all positions are covered.
- *Consolidated part time* will be a possibility in the next fifteen- to twenty-year time frame. This part-time program will exist for people who want to work a lumped-together time period throughout the year. For example, a person may want to work half time, but he may wish to work the first six months of the year and another person will work the last six months of the year. Of course, this part-time work will be rewarded with part-time pay.
- *Paternity/maternity leave* will replace the present exclusive maternity leave. Fathers will take time off to be with their babies just as mothers have in the past. Men and women may take joint paternity/maternity leave or may cycle it so that they are off at different times.
- *Civic/social sabbatical* will be a way to contribute to a person's civic responsibility and social life throughout a person's work life. McDonald's already gives employees time off at the rate of one eight-week period per ten years of full-time service. This contiguous time frame allows employees time to play, reflect, do civic work, or spend time with their families. Traditionally, employees have worked their total lives and have not been able to have this wealth of time until retirement. In the future, with more integrated lifestyles, companies will allow for flexibility and will have sabbaticals much akin to sabbatical leaves that the academic community has enjoyed for many years.[24]
- *Phased retirement* is already in experimentation in some organizations; e.g., Xerox Corporation. This will be more prevalent in later years as we find people doing more social work and having more integrated, balanced lifestyles. For instance, an individual may plan to retire five years from now and will work for eleven months in the fifth year away from retirement, the next year he will work ten months, and the next year seven months. Thus, the organization will phase the employee into retirement rather than suddenly have the person at work one day and off for the remainder of his life the following day.
- *Subcontracted employee labor* will be a work option as more and more workers become entrepreneurial and specialized and

as more companies pare down overhead in order to meet competition. It will be to the advantage of both the subcontracted labor and to the organization to have a hefty file of specialists on whom they can call for consultation in various areas. This option will increase productivity and cause increased profits among organizations in the future.

- *Individualized employee benefit plans* will also prevail as a result of changing demographics and increased automation. After all, why should both husband and wife of a dual-career family carry duplicate health benefits? In such a situation, one member of the two-income family might replace health care benefits with child care benefits if children are involved. The organization will consider holistic employee needs as opposed to merely servicing employee performance. Organizational leadership will become increasingly aware that physical and mental health, happy personal life, and reduced financial worries outside the organization will affect performance inside the company. A possible menu of benefits from which employees will choose are:

Health care benefits such as Health Maintenance Organizations, traditional health care insurance, dental insurance, optional maternity insurance, and wellness program bonuses;

Participative benefits such as deferred compensation plans (to hold down taxation and promote employee longevity) and stock ownership plans;

Legal reimbursement plans for help from lawyers and paralegals;

Child day-care total or partial reimbursement programs for care of children while one works or in-house day-care centers at work;

Financial planning reimbursement for work with licensed financial planning professionals in keeping one's money invested and intact;

Psychological and social counseling programs such as stress management, biofeedback programs, drug and alcohol abuse, marriage counseling, premarital counseling, as well as counseling for personal problems;

Health and fitness benefits such as on-the-premise gymnasiums, health club memberships, as well as company-paid time off to participate in such programs;

Hefty education reimbursement plans and constant retraining facilities on-site and in connection with local colleges and universities;

Elderly parent care with on-premises elderly care sites or reimbursed day-care centers for employee's elderly parents;

Shopping services or on-site computer catalogue shopping services such that employees during breaks can use their valuable time in shopping for everything from groceries to clothes.

High performers will be rewarded and "dead wood" will be "punished" under new performance-based systems. Employees will be treated much as athletes presently are. Each year (or some other appointed time frame) employees will interview for their present position just as they would any other position to which they are aspiring. Additionally, incentive systems will be structured to give bonuses to good performers throughout the year and to give no raises or bonuses for poor performance. Also, poor performers may even be fired as a result of this process. In the convulsive economy and in the face of competition, corporations will need to find creative ways to take a fixed pool of money and distribute that money to those who deserve it most. Such companies as Bank of America Corporation, General Motors, TRW Incorporated, Honeywell Incorporated, and Hewlett-Packard Company are already putting into practice these pay-for-performance reward systems. However, there are particular dangers of such a system in that these systems concern management fairness and judgment of performance. In a service and information environment, where productivity is difficult to measure, it is sometimes easier to be subjective than objective. In the future, new personnel performance measuring systems will be implemented to satisfy these future challenges.[25]

During the immediate future, companies will have increased liability for their work force, especially in cases of wrongful dismissal and age discrimination. More critical problems in the future will evolve from individual lawsuits against corporations than with collective union bargaining.–

Increasingly, workers are finding courts amenable to wider protection for employee rights. In April 1985, the Texas Supreme Court set a precedent. It ruled in favor of a worker who filed wrongful dismissal charges against his employer. The worker charged that he was dismissed after he refused to commit an illegal act. The Texas Supreme Court voted in the employee's favor and reversed a court precedent of ninety-seven years. Many states are ruling in favor of employees when the right to "fire at will" is in question. Another targeted point of employee liability is the area of age discrimination. Due to the aging work force, many employers are being sued today by individuals who have been laid off or dismissed and who feel that the dismissal was wrongful and totally based on age.

Between the years of 1980 and 1985, the number of people filing age discrimination lawsuits had almost doubled. In addition to that statistic, the Administration Office of U. S. Courts reported that 400 additional age discrimination suits were filed by individuals who did not act in concert with the government as did the other people heretofore reported.

An additional area of potential liability that will receive much future attention will be the area of employee mental stress, depression, and anxiety. Several lawsuits have already been cited whereby the plaintiff tried to hold the corporation responsible for his breakdown. For example, a widow sued her husband's former employer for $6 million, claiming that the company was directly responsible for her husband's death because they did not respond to his repeated complaints of overwork, and they then displayed a "callous and conscious disregard for his mental health." In another case, a California court upheld an award to a legal secretary who had a nervous breakdown and claimed that it was because of her heavy workload.

The Michigan Supreme Court awarded a monetary payment to a machine operator who claimed that he became mentally ill because of his daily work pressure on the assembly line.[26] More cases of this sort will continue as employees hold corporations more responsible for career satisfaction and mental health.

This liability will in turn cause corporations to be more conscious of direct and implied contracts. Corporations will become very cautious in their hiring practices. In addition, corporate liability insurance premiums will rise in the future at a much more rapid rate than in the past just as is happening in the field of professional liability insurance. At some point, the U. S. Supreme Court will intervene and perhaps suggest a ceiling on the amount of monetary award that can be granted under such conditions. This measure will save many companies from potential bankruptcy due to employee lawsuits.

CHANGING NATURE OF WORK

Picture yourself doing a job within the next fifteen years that is virtually unheard of today: for example, space geographer, biofarmer, teleconferencing coordinator, clone doctor, or solar array technician.[27] The future of America's job market follows along the line of a good news/bad news joke. The good news is that the Bureau of Labor Statistics estimates that in the next ten years 15.9 million new jobs will be created.[28] The bad news is that while new jobs are developing, many jobs will be displaced. The services sector will grow at an annual rate of greater than 2% in the next ten years, offsetting a greater than 2% loss in the goods producing industries of agriculture, mining, and manufacturing. Some industries of greatest growth will be health care, business services, computers, transportation, and plastics. Decline will be the trend in the following industries: cotton, timber, leather, iron, sugar, railroads, dairy, and steel.[29]

Some specific careers to avoid are:
Unskilled labor
College teaching
Farming
Private household employment
Machinist
Packer
Inventory control specialist
Typist
Postal worker
Traditional librarian
Clerk
Traditional telephone operator
Door-to-door salesperson
Railroad conductor
Assembler
Welder
Painter

Some careers of promise will be:
Registered nurse
Secretary
Truck driver
Janitor
Waiter/waitress
Computer scientist
Engineer
Technician
Electrician
Professional services salesperson
Technology salesperson[30]

Conclusion

By now you have probably concluded that our research indicates that the next fifteen years will be a time of transition. A business world very different from that of today will surround us. However, due to challenges that new technology introduces, you can see too that we have made conservative projections.

If these predictions do not fit your projections of tomorrow, then gaze into your own crystal ball involving areas of concern to you. List the forthcoming changes you envision and preliminary actions you must take.

Perhaps you will want to innovate your position. Convince your employer that the job you develop will be essential. Be creative! Be different! Finally, continue to read, absorb, envision, and school yourself. In the future, you must keep getting better in order to continue being good.

And remember, the key strategies for prosperity in tomorrow's business sector are:

- Anticipate
- Assimilate
- Innovate
- Educate

What an exciting world!

Summary:

1. Tomorrow's business world will be as different from today's business world as today's differs from the era of the Pony Express.
2. Overly optimistic projections can sometimes become perilous and fail to live up to predictions. Normally, conservative projections into the future are more dependable.
3. In general, tomorrow's business world will have a heavy influence of international culture, will be highly competitive and perhaps frustrating, fast paced, ever changing, and productivity oriented. Corporations will pare overhead as much as necessary to continue to service their customer base and, at the same time, produce profits in a highly competitive marketplace.
4. The physical work place layout will be transformed by high technology. Electronic work stations will take the place of many walled offices.
5. By the year 2000, 85% of U. S. workers will be in the trade and service sectors as opposed to manufacturing. Because of the transition to service, workers will be divided into two types: cognitive and substantive. Cognitive workers will be diversified further into Upwardly Mobile Professionals, Laterally Mobile Professionals, Downwardly Mobile Professionals, and Generalized Skills Professionals. Unskilled labor will be replaced by automation.
6. To compete in tomorrow's job market, the work force must be better educated and be continually trained to keep up with changes before they occur. By the year 1995, one-half of the U. S. population will have some college education.
7. The work force will be aging. By the year 2010, 50% of our general population will be over forty. By the year 2000, the median age of the U. S. population is expected to exceed age thirty-six. In 1990, 30% of the labor force will be forty-five or older.
8. In the New Age, organizations will be employee-driven as opposed to leader-driven as in the past. Rather than treat people as a disposable commodity, successful companies will treat their people as an economic necessity and will design programs and schedules around employee lifestyle needs.
9. The services sector of the work world will see at least a 2% annual increase of employment, whereas the manufacturing sector will witness at least a 2% annual decline in employment. There will be specific careers to avoid as well as specific careers of promise. In the New Age, people of wisdom and vision will seek to either train themselves for, or retrain themselves in, careers of promise.

Chapter 8

Develop Resource Connectors

> *No person is an island entire unto himself/herself.*
> —John Donne
> (paraphrased)

After surveying self-made millionaires, Thomas Stanley, Georgia State University marketing professor, discovered that the only common characteristic found among these materially successful individuals was a very thick Rolodex. Andrew Carnegie attributed his whole fortune to the power he received from a staff of approximately fifty advisers on the manufacturing and marketing of steel.[1] Henry Ford began his career as a poor, illiterate businessman and within twenty-five years had become one of the richest men in America. His greatest achievements came after he began associating with Thomas Edison, Harvey Firestone, John Burroughs, and Luther Burbank.

Andrew Carnegie and Henry Ford shared a valuable ticket to success—other people. We will call these people *resource connectors*. In his classic book, *Think and Grow Rich*, Napoleon Hill states: "Men take on the nature and the habits and the power of thought of those with whom they associate in a spirit of sympathy and harmony." A term often used today to signify that a whole is greater than the sum of its parts is the word "synergism." A group of people is synergistic because each person in the group can become more powerful through pooling resources and by borrowing from the resources of other people. As we discussed earlier, corporations are practicing this phenomenon today in order to establish their power positioning.

Because the New Age is an era of individual responsibility, "know who" will be more important than ever before. When you declare your independence and go into business with yourself, why not create a board of directors and advisers? The secret to being individually responsible is not from existing in total isolation, but in knowing who can connect you with the resources you need. However, you must initiate this process with people you select and not wait for them to find you. Deliberately seek people who can help you, and never forget to thank them for doing so.

You will need at least nine connector groups to prosper in the New Age:

1. Career
2. Role Modeling
3. Social
4. Shared Values
5. Intimacy
6. Self-esteem
7. Motivational
8. Professional
9. Spiritual

As we discuss each resource connector, think of at least three people who could fit into each group. Some people may even fit into more than one group, but don't expect one person to fit all resource connector needs.

CAREER CONNECTORS

Perhaps the most attention has been given to the resource connector, career. The importance of career networking has been espoused since the 1970s. "The most common reasons to start networking are to avoid isolation, to obtain current information in your field, and feel a sense of belonging in your profession," says Ann Boe, president of Career Networks in Carlsbad, California.[2]

Career networks have been around for many years but were not formalized. Formerly these groups simply met in gymnasiums, at club meetings, and at restaurants as they engaged in conversation concerning the company, its politics, and possible job openings. Information was exchanged. Much unrecognized power was pent up in these sessions. In the New Age, again it is your *know who* that can help you in any career from technical to sales, from blue-collar worker to gold-collar worker. Many of the good jobs

Develop Resource Connectors

will not be posted, but information about openings will be passed by word of mouth.

Formalized career networks will continue to mature as the need for more information materializes. With the growing need for education and training, these groups will be conduits of valuable information.

Career networks, however, need not be formal and have regular meetings. You can simply have a number of people on whom you may call to help you in a specific situation. Virginia S. sells software packages to banks. She makes a point to belong to as many bank associations as she can find. She develops good contacts and nurtures the business relationship. Virginia always volunteers for leadership positions and does an exemplary job in whatever she undertakes. This wins her admiration and puts her in the presence of leaders in the financial community. She regularly refers prospects to her banking colleagues, and, in turn, feels free to seek sales leads and referrals from them. Rarely does she make a cold call. Her production is great, and she wins many company sales awards. Virginia has mastered the art of career networking.

ROLE MODELING CONNECTORS

Too often a barrier is thrown in the way of success when we begin to contrast ourselves rather than to compare ourselves to others. Ricky G. approached me recently during a seminar break. He said, "I just don't understand. I have been trying to make it in insurance sales for several years. It seems that I have reached a plateau in income. I work hard but can't seem to earn more money than I did last year." He sighed, then continued: "What really disturbs me most is that Jerry W. entered the field just three years ago and has been an enormous success. I just know his income is much better than mine, and he doesn't work nearly as hard. Can you tell me what I am doing wrong?"

As I looked into Ricky's face, I could detect pain and frustration. I responded: "Since I don't know the whole story of you or of Jerry, I am going to speak from limited information. Given Jerry's meteoric success, let's compare your good points to his. Let's use Jerry as a role model. Perhaps we can find similarities that you can use to show what is right with you, not what's wrong." After spending the entire thirty-minute break comparing attributes, Ricky saw that he had a lot going for him, and that with patience he could have success similar to that of Jerry.

Role models are very helpful in any endeavor—family life, work, religion, and social circles. Though you would never want to be a clone, you can find the strengths of your role models and use them as guidelines for those characteristics you need in order to reach your goals.

An exercise I often have seminar participants do is to write down one major goal. Then, I have them list the positive attributes of someone who has already reached a similar goal. The only restriction placed on them is that the attributes listed must have contributed to the attainment of that goal. After that exercise, they then list their own positive characteristics. The participants then do a matching exercise—matching their positive attributes to those positive attributes of the role model. Many of those in the seminar are surprised to find that they already have many of the attributes that they need to reach their goal.

For example, one individual wanted to be president of his company. He chose a role model, the president of a similar company, and listed that role model's positive characteristics. Some of those traits he defined were good appearance, persistence, good communication, education, intelligence, and good contacts. The participant found that he had most of these characteristics already. All he needed to do was to refine his goal, establish a target date for accomplishment, redirect his career networking, and earn the position.

Mentors can also be your role models—and usually are. In addition to admiring them from afar, mentors can provide advice, guidance, and counsel for helping you attain your goals.

SOCIAL CONNECTORS

Psychologist Abraham Maslow in his classic pyramid of needs conjectured that people need a sense of belonging. After our physical and safety needs are met, we must fulfill our social needs. Maslow ranks social needs as even more basic and necessary than self-esteem and self-fulfillment. Few of us indeed could live isolated for any great length of time.

The New Age will hold the potential for separation and isolation. Telecommuters will find themselves seeking to be in the presence of others. Some people who have strong social needs may find it difficult to adapt to working in the home. These people will need the office environment. In the New Age, you may need to make a concerted effort to be with people. Make it a point to meet people for lunch or for some other occasion several times per week. If you associate with positive people, you will find your life more pleasant just from having been in the presence of such individuals.

SHARED VALUES CONNECTORS

Think of your best friend. Do you like this friend because he or she is like you or because this friend is different from you? Chances are the friendship bonded because of likenesses — of mutuality of shared values. There will be many ways to share values in the New Age. Religious values can be shared in a religious group of your choice. Hobbies can be shared with other individuals. For example, some of your most fulfilling moments may come from the time you spend in your art class. These people are able to relate to you on a personal basis and share your love for art.

In seeking out people like you, you will feel exhilaration and excitement. Joan D. was very close to her college roommate throughout their four undergraduate years. After graduation they went their separate ways and, although they lived within thirty miles of each other, rarely saw each other. Both married and had families and did not have much time for anything else but fostering their family relationships.

Then one day Joan called her former roommate Sandra and asked her to meet her for lunch. These two women rekindled the relationship they had experienced when they were younger. They found that they both enjoyed movies and could talk for hours about almost anything. In fact, the first time they met for lunch they talked until four o'clock and had not even noticed how rapidly time had passed. They then made an appointment to get together again the next week for lunch.

Week after week they began meeting to go to movies, theater, and ballet. Soon they discussed how guilty they felt because they were spending some time away from spouses and family. Each decided to discuss the situation with her respective husband. What surprised both of them was that their husbands had noticed a positive change in each of the women's lives. After their meeting, the women would come home vibrant and bubbly. They seemed more positive and enthusiastic about life. Their husbands insisted that they continue their socializing because it added to their marriage, and in no way took away from it. Joan and Sandra learned valuable lessons about value sharing. When we can associate with people who are like us, it adds to our life and increases the vivacity of living.

It is refreshing to meet with people who share ideas, beliefs, and interests similar to your own. Among sources for finding such people are trade associations, classes in continuing education, hobby courses, and your own family and circle of friends.

INTIMACY CONNECTORS

The ability to give and receive love is one of the greatest of all human needs. Psychological evidence points to the necessity of intimacy or closeness for normal human development. Written in 1692, *The Desiderata*, found in the old St. Paul's Church of Baltimore, poetically describes the universality of love:

> Be yourself. Especially, do not feign affection. Neither be cynical about love, for in the face of all aridity and disenchantment, it is perennial as the grass.

Erich Fromm believes that love develops from people's anxiety arising from separateness and their need to have an emotional union with other people. To maintain both psychological and physical health in the New Age, it will be important to have at least three people who can provide you with this closeness, intimacy, and love. Because families may live great distances apart and the number of children reared in one-parent households will increase within the next fifteen years, psychological balance can be maintained by deliberately establishing emotional closeness with several people. These multiple sources for intimacy will diversify your friendships and offer more varied sources for love.

Advice columnist Ann Landers took a poll in early 1985 by asking her readers to respond to this question: "Would you be content to be held close and tenderly and forget about 'the act' [of sex]?" To Ann Landers's surprise, more than 90,000 women responded to that question. "Yes" was the answer of 72% of the women who responded. They would be willing to be held close and treated tenderly and forget about the sexual act. Even more surprising than the response to this question was the fact that of the 72% who said "yes," 40% of those women were under forty years of age. In our fast-moving world, closeness is at a premium.

Menninger in *Love Against Hate* stated:

> Love is the medicine for the sickness of the world, a prescription often given, too rarely taken.[3]

Never could a truer statement be made about the New Age!

SELF-ESTEEM CONNECTORS

After your social needs are met, you need to feel important — to love yourself. Normally, self-esteem resource connectors are those people who know your abilities and are willing to verbally confirm them to you. These people may not be your good friends. They may be professional colleagues, employees, superiors, or peers. In building such a group, you surround yourself with people who are truthful with you and on whose judgment you can depend.

In the New Age with rampant, fast-paced change and intense competition, you will sometimes find yourself fatigued and may feel that your self-confidence is waning. In that case, you will call on one or more of your self-esteem resource connectors and relate to them your feelings about yourself. They will, in turn, reenergize you by reenforcing your competencies and will give you the strength to pick yourself up and continue on your road to success.

A high school senior track star demonstrated this principle one Saturday afternoon several years ago. He and his teammates had won the district championship and were now at the regional meet. The young athlete had trained and conditioned himself for this season and wanted more than anything to make it to the state finals for the climax to a great high school sports career. But first his team had to win the regional meet. The contest began. He heard the beginning gunshot and began to run around the track. He seemed to be doing quite well until he realized that he had lost concentration, was winded, and was experiencing muscle cramps. He ached and hurt to the point that he was considering leaving the race. At that time he looked to his right and saw his coach. He heard his coach yell: " . . . You can do it! You are capable of winning! Concentrate . . . concentrate! Relax! You're too uptight!"

Then the athlete began to think: "I am a star. I can do it. I'm capable. My coach says so . . . I CAN do it!"

After much hard pushing and self-talk, the track champion increased his speed until he eventually felt the tape break across his chest — signifying that he had won. What a day to remember! Just when he was losing confidence in his own ability, his self-esteem resource connector — his coach — took over reenforcing his self-belief. As a result, he went home a regional winner!

MOTIVATIONAL CONNECTORS

Quitting is easy; getting up, dusting yourself off, and trying again can be difficult. In the New Age this may be required of you a great deal. The major difference between winners and losers is the degree of motivation. Members of your motivation support group do not necessarily need to know your competencies as do your self-esteem group. They simply must believe in you.

A young child is often a motivator to his dad. With utmost faith the child believes that the dad can do anything. The child heroizes the parent. You too have people who believe in you. Of course, it is important that they tell you how they feel; often you must ask them in order for them to share their feelings with you.

When you are motivated, you move toward your goal with zeal and enthusiasm. No one else can motivate you, for that is an individual matter. However, they can provide an atmosphere that causes you to want to perform and to desire to do well.

Ellen J. was not a good student. Her grades were never above C level. She really did not believe she could do any better. Tests raised her anxiety level, and she just prayed to pass. Her alcoholic father always told her that she would not go very far in life and that she should just quit school and go to work. Her mother loved her but was so busy working to try to keep the family of six fed and clothed that she never had much time to spend with Ellen.

Then one day Ellen's speech teacher, Mr. Bingham, asked her to stay after school for a visit. That meeting changed Ellen's life. Mr. Bingham told Ellen that she had great potential as a debater and asked her to try out for the team. He pointed out that she had a very objective mind and was convincing in argument. Those qualities would lend themselves well to debate. He said: "Ellen, I believe in you. You have potential for a grand future in teaching, politics, or whatever you desire to choose as your field of interest. You can bring up those grades. I know you can."

That's all it took. Ellen skipped home that day—for the first time in her life feeling worthy and directed toward her dreams. Also, for the first time in her life she felt hopeful about her future. Mr. Bingham had given her one of the greatest gifts she could have received—his confidence in her.

The next semester Ellen made the honor roll. Two years later, she enrolled in college and majored in political science. Then she went to law school and became a prominent attorney in a time when few women were even entering the field of law.

She attributes her success to Mr. Bingham, her motivator, who took time to say: "Ellen, you can. I believe in you!"

Your motivator resource connectors may not approach you as directly as Ellen's did. You may have to search them out. Let them know that you need them to encourage you, to build you up, to write words of encouragement. You will be surprised how positively they will respond and how wonderful you will feel.

PROFESSIONAL CONNECTORS

From time to time in the New Age, you will need help in the areas of medicine, insurance, finance, law, taxes, investments, and general financial planning. It is important for you to select professionals in each of these areas who can help you. It is best to develop an ongoing relationship with a resource connector rather than have a new relationship every time you have a need. In order to establish professionals in each of these areas, you can check with appropriate associations for referrals as well as seek recommendations from friends.

When you are looking for a particular professional, interview these professionals as if they were applying for a job with you. In reality they are. Even though you may be calling on them and perhaps paying them a fee to see you, reserve the right to see other professionals in the area until you feel satisfied with the professional relationship established. Everyone needs a good physician who keeps a master health profile. Often we need financial specialists who can help us with particular needs. Insurance needs that cover liability, property, casualty, life, and health are necessary in order to combat some of the problems that we will eventually face. In Chapter 9 we discuss financial, insurance, and investment needs in more detail.

All people need a will and perhaps some estate planning. A good attorney specializing in that particular area can help save much time and worry when the need arises for will creation, probate, or estate settlement.

Tax information and advice can be handled by certified public accountants. They abide by a strict code of ethics and can serve your needs well in the tax area. Investment advice can be obtained from an adviser registered with the Securities and Exchange Commission or from a financial planner who also is registered with the SEC. As a conduit for investments, your broker will be helpful to you in maintaining your portfolio.

An additional group of resource connectors is community agents. For instance, you may need to find a nursing home for your elderly parents and have no idea where to turn. You might contact some of the agencies on aging in your particular area to serve as a conduit to your resource needs.

Material freedom in the New Age is spelled M-O-N-E-Y. Normally, most of our money is earned by working. However, sometimes we must borrow money to make purchases and investments. Bankers and other creditors are important resource connectors in order to secure loans when we need them. It is important to cultivate a professional banking and lending relationship. This financial relationship will be very important with the technical interconnectedness and deregulation of the New Age.

Establishing solid professional relationships is totally your responsibility. Make it a point never to be intimidated by professionals. Choose the professional who best meshes with your needs and personality.

SPIRITUAL CONNECTORS

In the quest for independence, people sometimes discover their vulnerability. At such a time, they realize they cannot live "by bread alone." They must believe in something more powerful than themselves. There are times in everyone's life when they feel out of control, and there are circumstances in life which we will never be able to control. People have always felt the need to connect to a supreme being for their inner peace. Religious sentiment is not only a fortification against fear, it also provides one of man's basic needs which is totality of "being." Psychologist Gordon W. Allport has aptly described mature religious needs:

> While religion certainly fortifies the individual against the inroads of anxiety, doubt, and despair, it also provides the forward intention that enables him at each stage of his [development] to relate himself meaningfully to the totality of Being.

Most all successful people in America believe in a supreme being—and consider that entity an important partner in every walk of life. Abraham Lincoln publicly announced that he made no major decisions about the nation before he first prayed for God's guidance.

One of the most beautiful messages that President Ronald Reagan sent to the American people was in eulogizing the seven

Develop Resource Connectors 123

astronauts who perished aboard the Challenger in January 1986. Quoting from the sonnet, "High Flight," by John Gillespie Magee, Jr., President Reagan said, "We will never forget them nor the last time we saw them this morning as they prepared for their journey and waved goodbye and slipped the surly bonds of earth to touch the face of God." [4]

It is important to establish for ourselves a spiritual support group who shares similar spiritual values. The New Age is filled with so many insecurities — the convulsive economy, career upheaval, lifestyle changes — that we often feel the need for a higher power that offers consistency to our lives.

People in our spiritual connector group will help to sustain us in "down" times and will share and reenforce the "up" times of our lives.

Conclusion

Important to us in the New Age will be resource connectors. Without them we have the potential to exist in isolation. Technological interconnectedness is not enough. Computers can never replace an individual's need for other human beings. In the New Age, however, people will not as readily come to us. We will be scattered in loose networks of facilities as opposed to closeknit groups of people in an office environment. Therefore, it is more important than ever before that we initiate groups of people on whom we can call. As we will discuss in Chapter 10, relationship-building techniques are important so that we know how to reciprocate to meet other people's needs.

Summary:
1. Most successful people share a common characteristic: they make valuable use of resource connectors, i.e., people who can help them.
2. There are at least nine resource connectors that will be helpful to establish in the New Age:
    Career
    Role Modeling
    Social
    Shared Values
    Intimacy
    Self-Esteem
    Motivational
    Professional
    Spiritual
3. You must initiate your resource connectors. They will not readily come to you.

Chapter 9

Prepare For Predictable Uncertainty

Success is to be measured not so much by the position that one has reached in life as by the obstacles which he has overcome while trying to succeed.
— Booker T. Washington

In today's highly integrated world economy, it is difficult to make economic predictions. Because economics is a social science, it does not lend itself to an exact mathematical framework. Instead, it follows human experience. People are complex and human behavior is less than predictable. The best that economists can do is to try to outguess human expectations and experiences based on similar circumstances from the past.[1] Because the New Age is different from our past, it is difficult to expect past economic patterns to totally repeat themselves. Therefore, due to new patterns of behavior and new forces of world economic order, the only safe prediction to make about the New Age is: *uncertainty will prevail.*

Until we collect enough data to predict global cycles, we will be making up the rules as we go. Preparing to live with predictable uncertainty is a challenge at its best. With the convulsive economy and global competition pressing our current economic structure, we must do the best we can to prepare for future situations.

With predictable uncertainty, security becomes a priority. All people define "security" differently. For some it means a stable job; for others, money in the bank; for still others, it is a big suburban house and a nice car — both debt free. Certainly, security is more a state of mind than a defined amount of money. You can feel relatively secure in the New Age if you can adequately handle potential crises that might occur.

The general economy, because it is convulsive, will have simultaneous ups and downs.[2] It is important to have the peace of mind that comes from knowing that you can not only survive but also prosper under these conditions. The seven economic conditions discussed in Chapter 4 will affect each person differently. Rather than plan for the economic impact on the masses, as is often the case, it is helpful for you to anticipate the critical events in your life and to plan how you will handle each situation when it occurs. For instance, a mass recession may not affect you as adversely as a job loss in a mass inflationary period. The key to economic prosperity in the New Age will be to determine how each of these life events affects you as an individual and to plan on an individual basis for these happenings should they occur.

In the New Age, happiness is most often defined as peace of mind. Although money does not buy happiness, it does contribute to your overall "peace of mind." Having adequate money for security is like *not having pain*. Only when you lack an adequate amount do you notice how much you hurt. Money allows more freedom of choice and alleviates survival worries in your life. Only when the pursuit of financial gain becomes an end in itself, to the exclusion of other sources of happiness, does it negatively affect your quality of life. In the New Age, money is the primary means of exchange for freedom and security.

A crisis is nothing more than an unexpected event for which you did not prepare. Critical events, which have been anticipated and planned, merely become unpleasant happenings. Although they may be tragic and heart-breaking at the time, they are not as devastating as when you have made no preparation for them.

These potential crises can be termed Probable Life Events (PLEs) in that you will be forced to face many of them during your lifetime. Here are ten possible PLEs:

        1. Career interruption
        2. Disability
        3. Property loss
        4. Liability lawsuit
        5. Marriage/Remarriage
        6. Children's college

7. Divorce
8. Retirement
9. Aging parents
10. Death

It is typical of human nature to think that tragedies all happen to someone else. Somehow you and I feel that we can escape life's big traumas. Often though, fate finds us and strikes.

The *Titanic* was not supposed to sink. In mid-April 1912, she set out on her maiden voyage from England to America. Because safety standards in those days were minimal, there were not enough lifeboats on board for the 2,200 passengers. Instead of having the required forty-eight lifeboats, the *Titanic* had only sixteen. The crew and owners felt no need to add more lifeboats because they simply took up too much room and, after all, the *Titanic* was built never to sink.

The captain was warned that he was in severe waters — that there were icebergs ahead. He was asked to decrease his speed; however, because the *Titanic* was not designed to sink, the warning was ignored. The *Titanic* collided with an iceberg and sank. On that mid-April day in 1912, there were only 300 survivors, mostly women and children, of the total 2,200 people on board. Through improper planning and failure to face the idea that a disaster might occur, many lives were lost. The *Titanic* story seems to have happened so long ago that we feel almost certain that such a tragedy would not occur again.

Two months ago I was on a cruise. During the boat drill, I routinely tried on and adjusted my life jacket just in case a potential problem might occur. Along with the other passengers, I laughed and joked about how this situation could never occur on today's cruises. I really did not believe anything would happen, although I would have been prepared for a mishap. As I suspected, my cruise went smoothly, and I returned home safely.

Four days later, on its very next cruise, that ship collided with another boat. All passengers were forced to don their life jackets and to flee in lifeboats. Luckily, the cruise ship lines had prepared them during the boat drill for just such an incident. No lives were lost.

Catastrophic events *can* happen today. They can happen to ships, planes, cars, and to you financially.

YOUR FINANCIAL PROFESSIONALS TEAM

Peace of mind comes not from avoiding life's potential problems but from positively planning for them. To prosper in the New Age, it is essential to first plan for the PLEs before planning for luxuries. As discussed in Chapter 8, developing a team of financial professionals for input to your planning process is important. Your financial team will consist of several of the following:

- financial planner
- attorney
- certified public accountant (CPA)
- insurance agent/s representing health, life, disability, liability, property, and casualty insurance lines
- banker
- trust officer
- stock and real estate broker

You may not need all these people, but you will probably need at least an attorney, CPA, insurance agent, and banker. It is essential to establish a good, sound professional relationship with these professionals in order to develop a financial structure that will aid you in surviving the convulsive economy. Many people simply have one professional to help them with all professional activity. However, if your income is above $65,000 per year, it might be better for you to consult a team of professionals — each specializing in his or her own field. It is difficult for any one person to be competent in all fields of financial and legal planning. It is better to get team input, not only for balance of advice, but also for more educated advice. The roles of most of these financial and legal professionals are obvious in your financial life.

The professional that is least restrictive and newest in the field of financial planning is the professional financial planner. Many people feel that a financial planner will magically solve their problems. No matter how good this professional is and no matter how much the fee becomes, no financial planner can totally solve your problems. You must also be involved in your own financial planning.

If you decide to use a financial planner, it is important that you seek a reputable one. There is no specific credential nor code of ethics by which all financial planners are asked to abide. In 1984, there were approximately 200,000 planners in the United States with training for this profession ranging from none at all to courses and a series of exams administered by the College for

Financial Planning in Denver. Brokerage houses will be able to offer training while many financial planners also hold credentials such as CPA, J.D. or M.B.A. Anyone can hang out a shingle as a financial planner. It is your responsibility to seek a reputable financial planner who will operate honestly and sincerely for your best interest.

There is a tremendous need for good financial planners. The International Association of Financial Planners estimated that in 1983 approximately $147 billion were being managed by members of that organization. In 1982, SRI International of Menlo Park, California, conducted a study and found that 5% of all U.S. households and 21% of households with a total income of $67,000 or more were using financial planners. Estimates state that as many as ten million American households could probably use financial planning advice.[3]

It is essential that an attorney help you draft such legal instruments as wills, trusts, powers of attorney, and contracts. People sometimes hesitate to seek legal advice because of the cost involved. However, the cost in the long run is sometimes much more than if they had consulted an attorney in the first place.

A good certified public accountant can help you with tax and accounting advice. If you have questions concerning tax shelters, the best way to take retirement benefits, or other topics in the realm of the CPA, it is usually worth the expense to seek the advice of this professional.

There is no substitute for an informed insurance agent representing a reputable insurance company. Often many of the Probable Life Events can be covered by insurance. You should check the credentials of an insurance agent and be certain the agent has your best interest in mind rather than just the commissions.

Education level in the insurance business can be obtained through various certifications. In the health, disability, and life insurance fields, one who has earned a chartered life underwriter or CLU has taken a series of courses and passed exams to develop a specific expertise in that field. The same holds true for the property and casualty agent. A series of courses and exams must be taken and passed for the agent to achieve a CPCU, chartered property and casualty underwriter, designation. When dealing with insurance agents, you should check out the companies they represent. Every large public library should carry a copy of *Best's Insurance Reports*. These directories rate the soundness of insurance companies. You will want to deal with a company rated A+.

Your banker, savings and loan, or credit union officer is an invaluable resource for you. There will be times in your life when you will need loans to help you through some problem or to make purchases on which you would rather not spend your cash. By setting up a good relationship with one or all of these professionals, you can have a lifetime source for money. Always make certain that you pay the money back on time or even before the loan is due. A clean credit rating can be your best asset.

Another professional, which may be your good fortune to meet, is a trust officer. When caring for aging parents, planning for your children's college, planning for your own disability, or doing transfer tax planning, your trust officer can advise you on ways you can use specific services to maximize your dollars and use them for your family instead of sharing them with the U.S. government. Although trust agreements are drawn up by attorneys, your trust officer can be an invaluable asset in the administration of your property at specific times in your life.

A broker, which is a salesperson for various investment vehicles, operates on either full or discount commission. A discount broker operates on a lesser commission than a full-service broker. Depending on the depth of your knowledge about investments you intend to make, you can consult either the discount or full-service broker. You must decide which one will best meet your needs. Real estate brokers can help you with your real estate purchases, and stock brokers can help you with purchases of mutual funds, bonds, stocks, limited partnerships, and other investments offered to the public.

In the New Age, total dependence on professional advice will not be enough. You must develop your own financial finesse, i.e., become familiar with terminology, types of investments, and be able to intelligently discuss the pros and cons of suggestions made by a professional. In the long run, you are individually responsible for your own financial growth and must be able to make critical financial decisions with valuable input from these professionals. You and your adviser will first see that you are adequately covered for the PLEs, then you can work together on an investment plan for surplus growth and additional prosperity.

NEW FINANCIAL RULES — NEW MONEY ATTITUDES

You can develop a greater peace of mind by incorporating a New Age money attitude into your investment strategy. Today most people continue to cling to the material attitudes fostered in the Second Wave Economy and have not yet been able to adapt to the strategies for the use of money in the New Age. When these New Age money attitudes are incorporated into your investment strategy, you will begin to see New Age prosperity in action.

Typical Second Wave money attitudes that people continue to possess today are:

- Consumption and spending are major economic goals.
- High income defines wealth.
- Income will increase each year up until retirement.
- Buy now, pay later.
- Repay debt in dollars of lesser value due to inflation.
- Use other people's money to leverage large purchases; i.e., borrow heavily for such investments as real estate and depend on the asset to increase in value at a greater rate than the interest on the loan.
- Depend heavily on tax shelters for wealth building.
- Become highly dependent on corporation and government benefits for personal security.
- The economy is stable and all debts can be repaid.
- Invest in such things as gold, real estate, and tangible equipment for greatest growth.
- Speculate with high risk to get rich quickly and invest in self and human resources last.

Since there are redefined financial rules in the New Age, those who prosper will change their thinking about money and investment and will incorporate a new set of financial strategies and New Age attitudes. The following are suggested ways to think about money in the New Age.

- Productivity and savings are major economic goals.
- Investment, not income itself, is a conduit for peace of mind.
- When you define enough money to support your lifestyle and work toward that goal, you will have more peace of mind than continuing to acquire material wealth without possessing a reason.
- Make as many cash purchases as possible. Keep debt payments below 15% of take home pay. This debt structure does not include mortgage payments.
- Depend less on inflation for asset growth and more on actual productivity and bottom-line performance.
- Depend on yourself and not outside sources for wealth building.
- Income will vary with corporate performance, career inter-

ruption, and convulsive economy. Next year may not always be as good as this year.
- For greatest growth, invest in yourself and human resources first, financial assets second, and tangible assets third.
- Prepare for probable personal crises in your life before investing in luxury items.
- Peace of mind develops from always living just below your means rather than equal to or greater than your means.
- Prosperity is built slowly over time by investing the surplus of your income over and above your lifestyle. "Get rich quickly" has been replaced by "get rich slowly."

PROBABLE LIFE EVENTS (PLEs)

PLE #1. CAREER INTERRUPTION

Though long-term career goals are commendable, long-term careers are rapidly disappearing. And there is no commercial insurance against job loss. You must self-insure. The most you could expect from career interruption is unemployment compensation plus possible collection of severance pay, vacation time, and some sick time. Economic conditions may make not only job change but also career change advisable. Although many new exciting careers will emerge, a period of retraining will be needed in order to convert to these new procedures and expectations.

Another economic condition promotes the possibility of career interruption: competition. Because companies are striving hard to survive in the face of the greatest competition ever, record numbers of mergers and acquisitions are taking place to increase corporate strength. Every day, approximately eleven mergers and acquisitions take place impacting the careers of all employees. Some careers will be improved, but others will be temporarily interrupted while the worker seeks employment elsewhere.

As a safety net for career interruption, keeping the equivalent of twelve months' expenses available is helpful so that you can have time to make a satisfactory career transition. The money should be invested conservatively and safely because this is your cushion against job loss. If your income is $60,000 or less per year and your age is forty-five or younger, it will probably take you on the average of one month per $10,000 in salary to relocate to another equivalent career.

For salaries above $60,000, it is more difficult to replace that position because of high-income level and fewer openings. For people over age forty-five, job relocation takes longer. So just to be safe, the twelve months' expense equivalent will provide you with peace of mind while looking for another job.

Having this year's expense cushion also will help you to create a more positive attitude. You will feel less desperate knowing that you have flexibility in choosing your next job. Your self-esteem will be enhanced, and those interviewing you will detect your confidence. Being desperate for a job is obvious and could negatively affect your chances of getting the position for which you are applying. Greater confidence is created when you know you have alternatives, and a cushion of money helps you to buy time to consider those alternatives.

Research indicates that displaced workers suffer a great deal of stress. The resulting pressure causes higher alcohol use, drug abuse, and family problems. Financial strains can cause feelings of desperation, loss of self-esteem, and even contemplation of suicide.

Rather than become a victim of the New Age corporate world with its paring for leanness, mergers, and acquisitions, you can prepare ahead of time and thus become a victor.[4] There is ample opportunity for those who seek it. Never before in history have so many exciting career challenges blossomed on the horizon. The secret to success is to be prepared to avail yourself of these choices, to be able to retrain, and to always maintain flexibility in career transition. Having a healthy savings account invested wisely and safely can take you far in peace of mind and self-esteem.

PLE #2. DISABILITY

Raymond J. had everything going for him — a beautiful home, automobiles, wife, and two lovely children. Sometimes he wanted to pinch himself to see if all this was real. Dental school had been difficult, and at times finances had been questionable. Then, after ten years of hard work, his orthodontics practice was thriving. One day without warning, he became nauseated. At first he thought he had a "bug." The nausea continued for several days, and he decided to see his physician. After several tests, he was diagnosed as having colon cancer. He is now undergoing chemotherapy and practicing his dentistry only on a very limited basis.

Cynthia C. was a forty-two-year-old career woman. She was admired by all her friends and family because of her meteoric rise to success in real estate sales. She seemed to be a natural salesperson and was good at turning prospects into clients. The

Prepare for Predictable Uncertainty 133

sky was the limit for her sales career. She decided to go to a real estate convention in New York last September. On the way back home to Los Angeles, the plane crashed. She was one of only three survivors and was burned over 50% of her body and paralyzed from the waist down due to a spinal cord injury. Her life changed drastically in a matter of seconds. She is now in daily physical therapy hoping to eventually regain the use of her legs. She must continue to undergo multiple surgeries for the restoration of skin and to rebuild her badly burned chest and facial areas. Her sales career is now "on hold."

Greg F. has worked for IMX Training Corporation for five years. His job is exciting and takes him all over the world. At social gatherings he is always the center of attention because he lives such an interesting life and has met such interesting people. Last week, Greg was at the wrong place at the wrong time. His plane was hijacked to Cuba, and he is being held hostage along with twelve other passengers and crew members aboard the jetliner. All other passengers and most of the crew were allowed to return to the United States.

Greg's wife is in a quandary. She has not slept for five nights. Besides intense worry over Greg, she cannot execute any of his business. They were in the process of selling their house when the hijacking occurred. It is time, also, to roll over Greg's IRA. It seems that the hijacking would be enough. However, her problems are compounded because she is not able to conduct his business. Greg's accounts, the house sale, and his IRA are all being held up indefinitely.

Raymond J., Cynthia C., and Greg F. all have something in common: disability either through sickness, accident, or temporary detainment. Although each situation is tragic, life could have been made easier through proper financial and legal planning.

Disability is not prejudiced. It strikes without regard to race, color, creed, age, or religion. If fate singles you out, then the results could be devastating.

Your chances of becoming disabled during your working years are three times greater than your chances of dying. Most disabilities last over ninety days (except temporary detainment). Sickness and accident disabilities have a median length of five years with some lasting fifteen years or more. If the disability allows you to continue working, but on a reduced schedule, the Social Security Administration reports a median income level drop of 62%. For forty-year-olds, it is projected that 28% of that population will suffer a disability before age sixty-five; for thirty-year-olds, twenty-nine out of one hundred people will suffer a disability before age sixty-five.

Perhaps one of your greatest blind spots in the New Age could be lack of preparation for temporary or permanent disability. As you increase travel, stress level, and risk brought about by New Age lifestyle, you increase your chances of disability. Perhaps this catastrophic problem, in some ways, is worse than death. You continue to consume, but discontinue to produce. Expenses of living normally rise. Medical necessities often outpace inflation.

You would need to be rich indeed to have enough assets to cover a major disability. Though you will be responsible for a portion of expenses, you can hedge your expenses of disability by obtaining an excellent quality of insurance coverage and by working with your attorney to obtain proper legal paperwork.[5]

Disability insurance

If you have 80% of total monthly income covered by disability insurance, and other sources, you are well covered. In fact, it is difficult to obtain more coverage. To determine if you are adequately covered, execute the following steps:

1. Add up all present annual expenses.
2. Divide annual expenses by twelve to obtain average monthly expenses.
3. Add up all annual expenses that you would incur if you were disabled.
4. Divide annual expenses if disabled by twelve to obtain average monthly expenses if disabled.
5. Compare your answers from Steps 2 and 4 to determine the larger amount.
6. Figure annual income from all sources that you would have coming in if you were disabled.
7. Compare Step 6 with present income to determine if there would be a shortage.
8. Compare the answer in Step 6 to Step 3. Is income if disabled equal to or greater than expenses if disabled?
9. Will income from all sources if disabled escalate with inflation? Is this income designed to last until you are age sixty-five?

After determining the amount of coverage needed, you then familiarize yourself with disability insurance definitions. By understanding these definitions, you will be better able to select a policy that best fits your individual needs.

Definition of disability: This definition indicates when you would collect full or partial benefits. Some definitions are very strict indicating that benefits will not be paid if you can work anywhere. A more liberal definition of disability is that benefits can be collected if you cannot engage in your own occupation. A medium-range definition of disability is that you can collect benefits if you are unable to engage in any occupation for which you are reasonably fitted by education, training or experience with due regard to your vocation and earnings prior to the occurrence of your disability — which would be either accident or sickness.

Non-cancelable: Under this condition, your insurance policy can neither be cancelled by the company nor the premium rate changed by the company.

Guaranteed renewable: A policy that is guaranteed renewable indicates that the policy cannot be cancelled, but the premium can be raised on the policy if all people's premiums in your classification are raised at the same time.

Participating vs. non-participating policy: A participating policy shares in any dividend surplus that the company pays. In a non-participating policy the profits would be paid to the stockholders instead of the policyholders.

Beginning date (or waiting period): This denotes either a specific date or specification of a time period in the number of days or months that you must wait before benefits would begin.

Benefit period: This length of time indicates how long your benefits will be paid. Most of the time, the "benefit period" is specified in number of years or until a specific age, such as age sixty-five. Some policies specify a benefit period of *life*.

Total disability: This definition normally coincides with the definition of disability listed earlier. This section defines the conditions under which you will be determined to be totally disabled and will be able to collect full benefits.

Presumptive total disability: Under certain conditions you will be presumed to be totally disabled and can collect full benefits even though you continue to engage in an occupation. Some companies will cover the loss of sight in both eyes, loss of use of both hands or of both feet, or loss of use of one hand and one foot as if you were totally disabled. In addition, many companies will cover the loss of speech or hearing under presumptive total disability. If this particular clause is included in your insurance policy, there is coverage of these conditions as if you were totally disabled. Often coverage of these benefits is paid from the first day of disability instead of after a waiting period.

Proportionate benefit: Sometimes people sustain a bodily injury from accident or become ill and are never totally disabled. They can work part time. Quite often a proportionate disability benefit will pay for a percentage of the total disability on the beginning date of disability whether or not the person has been totally disabled. Companies who do not pay a proportionate disability benefit normally require that a person be totally disabled before they can collect disability benefits for partial disability. Companies who offer the proportionate disability benefit have a more liberal payment plan than if they offered benefits simply for residual disability, which is a partial disability occurring only after a total disability has already occurred.

Separate periods of disability: This section of an insurance contract defines how long you must be back at work before the recurrence of the disability and before benefits will start over. If you have collected for a full benefit period, for instance, five years, then you may have to be back at work on your job for six months before the company will again pay for the recurrence of the same disability. Separate periods of disability vary among insurance companies.

Cost of living rider: Under this contract, the policy is indexed to inflation and premiums will keep up with a designated percentage figure of inflation as it occurs.

Additional death benefit: Under this contractual arrangement, you may increase the amount of coverage at specific time intervals without an insurance physical if you have the amount of earned income from work to support that increase.

Incontestability clause: This is a clause in your insurance contract which states the time limit after which the insurance company may not contest the validity of your contract. For instance, most incontestable clauses are either one or two years. Until that period has elapsed, the insurance company has the right to question your eligibility for the insurance in the first place and to question your direct disclosure of your condition on the application.

Waiver of premium: If your insurance policy contains this option, then after you are disabled for a specific amount of time specified in the policy, you will no longer be responsible for premiums on the policy which is paying you disability benefits.

Prepare for Predictable Uncertainty 137

Keep in mind that Social Security benefits have a very strict interpretation of disability and that it is difficult to qualify for these benefits. Rules for receiving Social Security benefits are:

1. Your condition must prevent you from doing any gainful work.
2. Your condition must be terminal or must be going to last for at least twelve months.
3. There is a five-month waiting period before any benefits are paid.[6]

After educating yourself to disability needs, you may shop for the best policy that will be in line with the coverage that you want as well as the premium that you wish to pay. You will want a stable company rated A+ by *Best's Insurance Reports*, which can be found at your local public library. You will want to be certain that your financial needs are covered until you can convert to a retirement plan or return to work, whichever occurs first.

You may be covered by your employer's group disability plan. If you do not understand the contract, ask your company employee benefits personnel to explain it to you. Make sure that you are satisfied with the coverage. If supplemental coverage is needed, then you can shop for a supplemental plan. Check to see if you have short-term coverage also, i.e., coverage for the first six months before long-term disability payments start. Some people are surprised to find that they fall short of this time frame and would be totally uncovered for several weeks.

If you are covered by a complete disability plan at work, you will not be allowed double coverage by other insurance companies. However, if your company policy's definition of disability is not as liberal as you would like, but your employer pays your premiums and you do not wish to withdraw from your group program, then you will not be allowed disability coverage from a private insurer even though you would be willing to pay. If you see that your contract is not satisfactory, simply talk to your personnel department and a good insurance agent to find out what would be the best program for you in supplementing your needs.

Often there is a difference in the policy that you want and the amount that you can pay for such a plan. Although you would probably want the best policy available, sometimes you cannot afford the total premium dollars. If there is a difference between your ideal coverage and the acceptable premium amount, at least do the following:

- Protect against major catastrophes. Be sure your coverage is guaranteed renewable and that benefits would be paid until retirement age.
- Accept longer waiting periods up front and go for long-term coverage. Have enough savings to cover the short-term coverage. These considerations will then reduce your premium.
- Do not depend on anyone else's generosity to bail you out of your disability situation. Even if you have to tighten your belt to buy disability insurance, you will be better off depending on yourself rather than on other people for a rainy day.[7]

In the area of disability insurance, it is advisable to prepare for the worst and then expect the best.

Health insurance

Medical care expenses are increasing at a much more rapid rate than inflation. Most employers carry group plans on their employees, but it is the ultimate responsibility of the individual worker to determine if coverage is adequate. Employers may offer traditional health care insurance, Health Maintenance Organization membership (HMOs), or a Preferred Provider Organization (PPO).

For traditional insurance an adequate health plan might offer:

- Eligibility for you as an employee and your family, including dependent children and full-time students up to age twenty-three.
- Hospital room and board at the full daily rate for up to 120 days.
- Surgical expenses measured by an up-to-date schedule with a set maximum.
- Adequate payment after basic benefits are used up, which is normally a $100 deductible for each person in the family and a $200 family maximum deductible per calendar year, with payment at 80% of covered medical expenses after the deductible is met. A lifetime maximum of at least $1 million per family is suggested by professional insurance counselors.
- Conversion privileges to a private plan should you leave the company.
- Payment of full expenses or a high maximum in intensive or coronary care.
- Coverage for family members from date of birth such that any child born with a defect would be covered.[8]

If you feel that your company's health plan is inadequate, then you can check with several private insurers to get a high deductible amount and supplement your group coverage. Some policies carry a $6,000 deductible amount, others carry a $10,000–$25,000 deductible. Your company would pay the initial benefits, then your catastrophic insurance policy would take over at that point.

It is important to be satisfied with your health care benefits. It is also important to check your health care benefits to see if they will cover new high-technology surgeries and implants. For instance, if you need an artificial heart, would that be covered in your plan? Do not wait until you need insurance to become familiar with terms of coverage.

If you have no group coverage at this point, then you may check with several private insurers to obtain a personal plan that will include the adequate coverage that we have mentioned earlier.

Companies with twenty-five or more employees and a health plan are required to offer a prepaid group plan if approached by a qualified HMO already in existence. HMO members pay a flat monthly fee regardless of how much medical care is administered. Under traditional health care plans, you normally get to pick your doctors. Under most HMO plans, however, a group of predetermined physicians attend you. There is a type of HMO where you can have the advantage of an HMO without having to give up your personal physician. If your personal physician joins an Individual Practice Association, you can prepay for his services just as you would in a regular HMO. However, you and your personal physician must locate facilities from which to administer the health care.

In twenty states, Preferred Provider Organizations now exist. PPOs point employees to groups of health care providers who will agree to a predetermined plan. This serves to keep costs down. Normally, doctors and hospitals have been contracted to your insurer and employer at discount rates. These providers, because a higher volume of business is steered to them, can provide your health care at a less expensive rate. With HMOs and PPOs, you should be certain to check your contractual agreement to determine what your coverage would be should you become ill in another town or another country.

If you are sixty-five and are eligible for Medicare, you will probably need a Medicare supplement. Information on Medicare and how to choose a Medicare supplement can be obtained free of charge from your local Social Security office.

Other special types of health care plans can be purchased from your insurance agent. Specific coverages such as dental coverage, cancer policies, and in-hospital payment insurance are available. Before availing yourself of any of these policies, you should first have excellent major catastrophic coverage. You should seek the advice of your financial planning and trusted insurance professionals before purchasing any of these insurance policies. It could be that you are covered for major catastrophic illnesses under the plan which you have today. Very few people are overinsured, but it is always best to make the most of the dollars put into your insurance policies.

Power of attorney and living trust

Accidents, sickness, and temporary detainment may render you unable to sign your own paperwork and/or transact your own business. In that case, someone would need authority to act for you. For several sets of circumstances, including those people who do not have enough assets to justify setting up a trust but who want to spare their families the trouble and expense of a petition for a court-supervised guardianship, power of attorney is a possible alternative.[9]

The power of attorney is a written document in which you appoint someone to act in your place. This person is known as your agent or your attorney-in-fact. The power can be very broad, allowing your agent to do anything you could do, or it can be limited, whereby you denote exactly the powers you wish your agent to have. In some states the power of attorney would end when you (the principal) become mentally unstable and would be unable to handle your own affairs. However, 75% of the states now allow a durable power of attorney that allows your agent to act for you throughout your mental incapacity until your death. The power of attorney ends at your death.

One warning that you should heed: the person you declare as your attorney-in-fact should be someone you trust. Remember, you are letting the agent do anything you can do if you allow a broad power, and you are letting the agent execute some amount of your business even if you allow only a limited power of attorney. You should seek counsel of your legal adviser to find the best way to set up a power of attorney and to put check points on the individual you designate as your attorney-in-fact.

Prepare for Predictable Uncertainty 141

Many individuals consider the living trust—known otherwise as the *inter vivos* trust. This is a more sophisticated instrument than a power of attorney. Normally, fees are generated for this type of instrument; therefore, your asset level needs to be large enough to justify the administration expense of such a trust. Your attorney and trust officer can advise you as to the minimum asset level required to justify setting up such an instrument.

A living trust would be created during your lifetime. You would be known as the grantor, and the one holding the property for you would be known as the trustee. Property would be held and managed for the benefit of another person known as the beneficiary. In a living trust, you may not only be the grantor, but you may also be the beneficiary.[10]

Reasons for setting up a living trust would include the following:

1. You want someone else to manage your property for you.
2. In the event of your death or disability, you desire continuity of property management.
3. You want more sophisticated investment advice.
4. You wish to guard against your incapacity to protect your own business, whether you are mentally, physically, or legally incapacitated.[11]

Other reasons for setting up such a trust exist. It is advisable to spend a great deal of time in legal counsel to determine the best way for you to set up such an instrument.

If Greg F.—whose plane (in our previous example) was hijacked to Cuba—had earlier set up a living trust or a power of attorney with his wife designated as trustee or attorney-in-fact, respectively, most of his business could have been executed whether or not he was present. As it stands, without those instruments Greg's wife can do nothing until he returns or until she goes through potentially time-consuming and expensive legal channels.

PLE #3. PROPERTY LOSS

Although you may have adequate savings and assets to support your lifestyle, loss of home and automobiles could greatly reduce your net worth if there were inadequate insurance coverage.

Loss to home and other structures

You might spend many years saving for your new home and beautiful furniture only to have a tornado demolish your treasures.

Adequate homeowners insurance will help to replace or repair those possessions without wiping you out financially. Under your homeowners insurance plan, two types of property can be covered — personal and buildings. Coverage will range from

- the basic form, which insures against perils such as fire and theft, to
- a broad form, which covers numerous items, to
- an all-risk type of insurance, which covers almost every possible kind of event (although some events, of course, are eliminated in all insurance).

Liability and medical payment insurance are also part of your homeowner coverage. Available are: personal liability that you might incur for each occurrence; medical payments to others up to a specified limit in case they are injured on your property; and coverage for damage you might do to the property of others.

In buying coverage for your homeowners insurance, you need to carry 80% of the replacement cost of your dwelling less the value of the lot and foundation. If you do not carry that percentage, then you would be responsible for a greater loss.

Something else to remember is the definition of *replacement cost provision* versus *actual cash value provision* of homeowners insurance. When your homeowners policy covers furniture, clothing, and most of your other belongings for actual cash value, it will pay you the replacement cost new less depreciation. An alternative kind of replacement value is replacement cost coverage in which items would be replaced with like kind and quality (or even replaced new) without considering depreciation. Some policies limit replacement under that provision to 400% of actual cash value.[12]

Often insurance contracts place internal limits on such items as money, jewels, furs, securities, watercraft, silver, and guns. You can read your homeowners policy to determine if you have items in these categories that are more valuable than the insurance company would reimburse if they were lost.

For example, coins and loose money that would be stolen out of your home are normally covered only up to a limit of $100. Jewels and furs may be covered up to $500. It would be easy to check your insurance policy to see what coverage you have. If the internal limits of these and other items are too low, then it might be advisable to talk with your agent about scheduling your property, i.e., listing the property and increasing the amount that would be paid for each item. Or you can carry something called a personal articles floater, which would be similar to a separate insurance policy insuring only that personal article.

For instance, your diamond engagement ring may not be covered adequately under your homeowners policy. You may wish to carry a personal articles floater which covers theft of your diamond ring. Scheduling the property and carrying a personal articles floater will increase your premium. You should discuss with your agent the increased premium versus how much loss you would sustain if these items were destroyed or stolen. Normally, to be eligible for homeowners insurance, the dwelling you insure must be owner-occupied. You may be able to obtain coverage for unrented seasonal dwellings. Your insurance agent will be able to help you with these items and with other questions you may have.

If you do not have a satisfactory homeowners insurance policy and you are in the market for other policies, then you may phone or visit several insurance representatives to discuss the necessary provisions of a policy for you. You may also consult *Best's Insurance Reports* for the A+ rated property and casualty companies.

If you own property other than your home, you will want to talk with your insurance agent about possible liability and other types of insurance for that property. Without proper insurance, you could be setting yourself up for tremendous losses not only to property but also liability losses through lawsuit.

Automobiles

Other than damage to your home and other buildings, your automobile leaves you open to large losses either by damage done to it or by it. Under your automobile insurance, there are six basic coverages:

1. Bodily injury liability will provide money to pay any claims brought against you plus the cost of legal defense if your car is involved in killing or hurting someone.
2. Property damage liability will provide money to pay claims plus defense costs if your car is involved in damage to the property of other people.
3. Medical payment insurance will pay medical expenses that result from injuries sustained by you, your family, and any other passengers in your car.
4. Uninsured motorists protection pays for injuries caused by either a hit-and-run driver or a motorist who causes damage to your automobile but does not carry insurance.

5. Collision insurance will pay for damage sustained by your car resulting from a collision or wreck involving your automobile alone.
6. Comprehensive physical damage insurance will pay for the damages when your car is damaged by perils other than collision. Examples of such perils under this coverage would be fire, hail, flood, or vandalism.[13]

If you live in a state that has "no-fault" auto insurance laws, you are required to carry personal injury protection (PIP). This protection pays reasonable and necessary medical expenses for the insured, family of the insured, other passengers in the automobile, and reimburses lost wages for a specified number of years, normally three.

Collision and comprehensive physical damage insurance usually carry deductibles, i.e., you pay a portion of the damage, normally $50, $100, $200, or $250, before the insurance company will pay for damages. You then are responsible for very small damages, and the insurance company contributes to payment for the more catastrophic problems.

As in other insurance, it is helpful to check *Best's Insurance Reports* for A+ rated automobile insurance companies. Since these basic coverages come in a package, you will need to compare prices for the whole package. Some companies will offer what is called a "deviated rate" in that they will give you a reduction off the premium before you pay it. Other companies offer a "dividend rate," which means that they give you a return of premium at the end of the year. When you are considering the two types of companies and the deviated versus dividend rate, consider the use of the money for the whole period of time in which you would not have use of it under a dividend reimbursement plan. Some insurance companies offer neither the deviated rates nor dividend reimbursement plans.

Often you can reduce the costs of your automobile insurance by having the highest possible deductible and sustaining part of the risk yourself plus taking a defensive driving course. Sometimes people over sixty-five may qualify for better rates simply because of their age and a good driving record. People living under the same family roof would find it less expensive to attach their cars to the family policy. Often there is a reduced rate if multiple cars are carried on the same plan. If you own a farm or ranch and keep a vehicle there, you may save money by classifying the vehicle for farm use if the vehicle is registered as such.

After their automobile is several years old, people sometimes drop the collision and/or comprehensive portion of their automobile insurance. Whether or not you can afford to do this depends on how much risk you can afford to take yourself.

It would be helpful to discuss all the insurance possibilities with your agent and to keep up to date on tax law changes that affect casualty deductions.[14]

PLE #4. LIABILITY LAWSUIT

Lois L. had saved money all her life to buy a small acreage on the outskirts of town. Finally, last year she was able to purchase a plot of land. She and her friends spent several weekends relaxing there. Then one Thursday evening a tragedy occurred. Three young people were driving along the road in front of her acreage and decided to climb over the fence in spite of the sign that said "No Trespassing." Upon discovering the pond, they decided to go for a swim. One of them dived into the pond in an area that was too shallow for his height. Lois L. is now being sued for $5 million, charging that she failed to post a sign denoting the depth of the water and the danger of the pond.

Though Lois is intensely worried, not only about her financial future but also about the injured youth, she feels somewhat relieved because she had attended a seminar the year before and had heard about extended liability coverage called an *umbrella policy*. Following the advice of the seminar leader, she obtained such a policy with a $10 million maximum. She feels fairly comfortable in knowing that should the plaintiff win the lawsuit, her liability would be covered under this plan.

Lois L. is not alone. Excluding payments ordered by judges plus out-of-court settlements, in 1982 there were 251 personal injury cases awarded by juries. The number increases every year. No one is exempt from lawsuit.

In order to protect yourself against large judgments against you, you might do as Lois did. You can buy a relatively inexpensive umbrella insurance policy. This type of coverage is also known as extended personal liability because it rises above your homeowners and automobile insurance to protect you against assessed damages. It protects you against physical injuries, libel, slander, shock, mental anguish, sickness or disease, false arrest, wrongful entry or eviction, malicious prosecution, defamation of character, and the list goes on. Of course, there are exclusions as in any insurance policy. Under a personal umbrella policy, business situations are not covered.

Another exclusion to check out in an umbrella policy is the coverage of volunteer service in the form of church work, charity, civic or condominium association board membership, or volunteer service activities. When doing such work, you should check to see that the organization has some liability policy that would cover you. The umbrella policy is relatively inexpensive, and financial planners usually suggest this coverage as routine for their wealthier clients. A million-dollar umbrella policy can be obtained for an annual premium that approximates the fee for one hour's legal defense. Umbrella policy coverage can be purchased in policy limits of multiple millions of dollars.[15]

If you do not own an automobile and/or a home and therefore have no auto or homeowners coverage, you can purchase a comprehensive personal liability policy. Just as in the umbrella policy, this particular plan does not cover business or professional liability. Separate policies must be obtained for those particular coverages. The comprehensive personal liability policy can be obtained with as little as $10,000 single limit up to multimillion dollars of single limits. This protects you in much the same way as the umbrella liability policy would.

Your property and casualty agent will be able to discuss these types of plans with you. Your agent will also be able to specify liability limits required on auto and homeowners insurance before the umbrella policy will take over. The comprehensive personal liability policy would not require underlying auto and homeowners insurance.[16]

By planning ahead for possible legal catastrophes that might wipe out your asset structure, you can have more peace of mind and can enjoy life better in the New Age.

PLE #5. MARRIAGE/REMARRIAGE

Although marriage is designed to be one of the happiest moments in your life, it can quickly turn to tragedy without proper prenuptial planning. Due to varied New Age lifestyles, two-career couples, the increase in divorce and remarriage where there are children by a former marriage, and the tagging of the value of contributions by homemakers, planning for marriage and management of assets is more important in the New Age than it has been in past economies.

Before your impending marriage, you should notify your professionals and advisers of the coming event. If your name will change as a result of the marriage, it is important to change business documents to reflect your new marital status. Some of the routine business to be executed is:

- Talk with insurance agents and employee benefits specialists to check for double insurance coverage and dispersion of pension funds.
- Notify the Social Security Administration of your marital status change in order to be eligible for spouse benefits in the future.
- Counsel with your attorney to determine if you need to rewrite your will, power of attorney, or trust instruments; and execute a prenuptial agreement.
- If you are changing your name, contact all necessary organizations that would carry identification on you: credit bureaus, drivers license bureau, and credit cards. If you change your name on credit cards, be sure they are cross referenced to your spouse after marriage if you wish cross-referenced credit ratings. Contact clubs and change your name on all employee benefits and paperwork. This list is not exhaustive. Only you will know wherein your name appears. You may not wish to change your name on all documents. Keep your former name on identification if you wish. Normally, keeping of the former name applies to women rather than men. However, in the New Age, it will not be unreasonable that men will change their name to the woman's in marriage or that the spouses will hyphenate the names. Simply do what is applicable to meet your particular situation.
- Execute all necessary financial paperwork, contacting all your investment advisers, banks, savings and loans, and credit unions to change necessary paperwork for stocks, bonds, financial service accounts, etc.[17]

More and more to-be-married couples are executing prenuptial agreements with one of the following goals in mind:

1. To protect inheritances of children
2. To clarify ownership of property
3. To disclose debts
4. To reveal financial obligations and promises
5. To define responsibility for support
6. To tag a percentage of a husband or wife's future earnings belonging to the spouse who worked to put that husband or wife through school to earn a professional degree.[18]

Courts in more than 50% of the states now recognize the prenuptial agreement. Your attorney can advise you of this contract status in your state. Before having your attorney design a formal agreement, gather the following data and discuss it with your spouse-to-be:

- All property you own — real estate and personal
- Pension plans and how they are to be handled upon your retirement and death. If your new spouse is not to receive benefits upon your death, then your spouse must sign a document with your employer stating that he does not want your benefits. Otherwise, your benefits will go to your spouse.
- Insurance policies — who will be beneficiary?
- Outstanding debts and credit card obligations
- Obligations to family members, such as aging parents, college education for children
- Amounts for the household budget and who is responsible for payment
- Obligations to any former spouse or spouses and children of former marriages
- Ownership of autos, boats, and other vehicles and luxury items brought into the marriage — will ownership be merged?
- Handling of future earnings or ownership of a business owned before marriage
- A personal expense budget including contributions to charity, clubs, and other personal expenses
- Terms and conditions of wills and disbursement of inheritances
- How to divide assets in case of divorce
- Investment and risk philosophy as well as who will manage the investments
- Provisions and consequences of breach of this prenuptial contract
- Dates and conditions for revision of the prenuptial contract.[19]

You may feel that discussion of these facts and the execution of such an agreement take the romance out of marriage. The opposite case is normally true. With this business cared for and out of the way, you can concentrate on the greatest rewards of marriage: love and mutual companionship.

PLE #6. CHILDREN

A cherished child is an awesome responsibility. The financial commitment even to one child can be mind boggling. In the New

Age, two-career couples are often waiting until they reach their early thirties and beyond to have their first child.

Even with proper planning, you may be surprised to discover the staggering expenses that accompany child rearing. The financial burden will be more pronounced on one-parent households. In 1982, female-headed households with one or more children under age eighteen numbered 5.9 million; and that number is increasing each year as the divorce rate and out-of-marriage birth rate soar.[20]

Family expenses will increase upon the arrival of a child in the areas of child care, food, clothing, shelter maintenance, additional activities in which the child participates, increased utility bills, increased insurance premiums, and maybe even larger housing. Teenagers' expenses run approximately 200% higher than those expenses incurred in the birth year.[21]

"Aside from a house, a college degree is likely to be the single most expensive outlay one makes in a lifetime," indicates The Research Institute of America report on college planning. Planning for your child's college should begin at the child's birth. By waiting until the child enters college, financial drain from income flow could reach crisis proportions. You can expect student aid if need is proven. Also, your child can work while in school to earn additional money. However, due to heavy New Age competition and increased pressure for excellence in education, your child may find it difficult to work very many hours and, at the same time, excel in school. The need for increased scientific and technical expertise will demand that college courses require more effort in the future.

College costs are expected to increase at the rate of 8% per annum throughout the 1980s. For the 1985–86 college year, it is estimated that tuition, fees, room and board, supplies, personal expenses, and transportation will be $5,314 at the average public four-year school and $9,659 at the average private four-year school. Chart 4 indicates the average per year cost in the years ahead, assuming an 8% education inflation rate.[22]

Year	Private College	Public College
1990	$14,189	$ 7,806
1995	$20,854	$11,473
2000	$30,638	$16,856
2005	$45,020	$24,768
2010	$66,145	$36,390

Chart 4.
Projected College Costs Per Year at 8% Inflation Rate

Your financial adviser will be able to direct you to techniques and tools for planning your child's college funding. Tax laws are ever changing in such a way that many of the vehicles used as we go to press may be questionable in the future. It is best to seek state-of-the-art advice on various trusts, custodial accounts, and zero coupon bonds available to help finance your child's education. Other vehicles than the ones we have mentioned are being made available all the time. It would be difficult indeed for middle-class families to depend only on systematic savings for total college funding.

PLE #7. DIVORCE

Just as severe as the emotional upheaval of divorce is its financial complexity. Normally, women do not fare as well after divorce as men. In most states the new equitable distribution laws cause women to end up with approximately one-third of marital assets plus all of their assets they owned prior to the marriage or were gifted to them or inherited by them after marriage. In the nine community property states (Washington, Idaho, Nevada, California, Arizona, New Mexico, Texas, Louisiana, and Wisconsin as of 1986), there may be closer to a fifty-fifty distribution of marital assets. At any rate, the divorce judge decides upon the asset split unless the divorcing couple can negotiate an agreeable settlement between themselves.

Economist Philip Robins conducted a study for the Social Security Administration and found that of the 2.3 million divorced women with children, only 36% were getting the support awarded them upon divorce. Only 53% were receiving anything that was awarded. Often it is better to get a big settlement up front than to rely on future spousal payments.[23]

Although no one ever expects his or her marriage to end in divorce, in reality divorce does occur in greater than 50% of today's marriages.

If an adequate prenuptial agreement is in order and has spelled out a division of property upon divorce, then this emotionally wringing event can be made much easier. The key is to have the prenuptial plan in place before marriage and certainly before divorce. This instrument may be one of the greatest lifetime gifts you will give to yourself.

Divorce can be expensive. Even if there is an amicable dissolution of property, there will be expenses involved. Since there is change in marital status, the same people must be contacted and paperwork executed that was discussed in the marriage/remarriage section.

If you are carried as a dependent on your spouse's health insurance, you will no longer be eligible as a divorced spouse. Difference in expense can be part of the dissolution agreement. Pension division should also be a matter of discussion — especially that portion acquired after marriage.

Though marriages may be made in heaven, many divorces can be made easier through logical negotiation in the lawyer's office.

PLE #8. RETIREMENT

Retirement planning should begin the day you start to earn income. In the era of individual responsibility, you and your personal investments will be the source of a great percentage of your retirement income — perhaps as much as 50–75%. Because Social Security is controlled by Congress and is subject to change, the exact amount of future benefits available may be questionable. If you are under a corporate pension plan, you will need to be cautious and not accept the availability of future funds with blind faith for these reasons:

1. Not all corporate plans are insured by the Pension Benefit Guaranty Corporation (PBGC). Only defined benefit plans (those promising a specific amount at retirement based on a formula for income and years of service) are covered, and coverage is limited. Therefore, you may not receive the amount of retirement pension money for which you had planned.
2. Most corporate plans are offset by Social Security payments which you will receive. The average corporate plan payment ranges from $300 to $400 per month.
3. Not all plans are adequately funded by the corporation, making future payments questionable, especially if the company goes bankrupt.
4. Most plans do not give cost-of-living raises after retirement begins. Within a few years of retirement, you begin to lose purchasing power.

In planning for retirement, you will answer the following questions.

- How much income will I need?

- To produce that amount of income, what asset level do I need to accumulate?
- How do I invest my money to meet my retirement goals?

Assessing income needs

First, make a list of all expenses you will incur in retirement. Do not forget to include insurance premiums and a health care supplement to Medicare if not furnished by your company. Express the amounts in today's dollar values. Then use the figures from Chart 5 to determine the effects of inflation on future expenses.

For example, Philip and Suzanne will retire in twenty-five years. They feel that they could maintain an expense level of $2,000 per month if they retired today. They also expect that inflation will average approximately 6% in the future. By consulting Chart 5, Philip and Suzanne find that they need to multiply $2,000 by 4.292 in order to determine the future amount needed by them in twenty-five years. Philip and Suzanne find, after their calculation, that they would need income of $8,584 to cover expenses per month ($2,000 x 4.292) twenty-five years hence. This figure is the amount needed during the first year of retirement. Inflation would then escalate the amount as the years go by.

Years From Now	Multiply Today's Expenses By
5	1.338
10	1.791
15	2.397
20	3.207
25	4.292
30	5.743

Chart 5.
Growth of Expenses at Inflation Rate of 6%

Asset level to accumulate

Determine the percentage of retirement income you can realistically expect from Social Security and your corporate pension plan. Remember to estimate conservatively in that the convulsive economy, competition, and targeted prosperity can trigger changes in laws and corporate stability over a period of years.

Subtract the percentage of income to be furnished from 100%. The remainder is the percent for which you are responsible. Then, multiply the percentage for which you are responsible by the

Prepare for Predictable Uncertainty 153

monthly expense amount necessary to support your lifestyle. Next, multiply your answer by twelve to determine the annual amount needed. Last, divide your annual amount needed by the expected rate of return to determine principal or asset level needed to generate your necessary income to meet expenses.

For clarification of the above formulae, let's continue with the example of Philip and Suzanne. They projected that they would need $8,584 per month in twenty-five years to equate to $2,000 per month in expenses today. They feel that Social Security and their company pension plans will provide 50% of their retirement income. Therefore, they must provide the other 50%. Using our formula previously discussed, Philip and Suzanne multiplied 50% by $8,584 to arrive at $4,292 per month that Social Security and company pensions would pay. They, then, are responsible for the other $4,292 per month. That amount multiplied by twelve equals $51,504—the annual amount of retirement income they must provide for themselves.

To determine asset level needed to produce this $51,504 per year, Philip and Suzanne would project an expected rate of return in twenty-five years. If they expect to get a 10% rate of return, they would simply divide $51,504 by 10% to arrive at the asset level required in the future. The answer is $515,040: i.e., Philip and Suzanne need assets of $515,040 yielding 10% to produce income of $51,504 per year. At this level they would never need to reduce the principal if returns remain at 10%. If the interest rate drops below 10%, they would have provided a safeguard for fund depletion in case they need to tap the $515,040 for emergencies or for additional income.

You can now project your own necessary future asset level by going through the same procedures as did Philip and Suzanne.

Investing for goals

Retirement may be the greatest long-range planning task you will ever undertake. Once you have determined the amount necessary for retirement, you then need to set yearly investment goals. Chart 6 will help you to determine these objectives. In Column 1 of Chart 6, simply find the approximate number of years you have until retirement. Then divide the amount you set as an asset level goal from our previous formula by the number in Column 2 of Chart 6 directly across from "years to retirement."

Years To Retirement	Divide Asset Level Needed in Retirement By
5	5.985
10	15.193
15	29.361
20	51.160
25	84.701
30	136.308

Chart 6.
Amount to Invest at the End of Each Year
Assuming a 9% Return[24]

To determine the amount they need to invest each year to retirement and assuming a 9% rate of return, again returning to our example, Philip and Suzanne would divide their $515,040 asset level needed by 84.701 (since they will retire in twenty-five years). They find that they must invest $6,081 at the end of each year for twenty-five years to meet their retirement goals.

Again you can apply your own numbers to this formula to determine your own yearly savings and investment objectives.

How to invest to meet your goals

One of the best retirement planning devices is the individual retirement account (IRA). You can deposit up to $2,000 per year in such a vehicle. After several years, your IRA will have accumulated into a sizable amount which can go a long way in furnishing your retirement income. Not only is the IRA an asset accumulation vehicle, it also offers a tax break.

All IRAs must be opened and funded by April 15 of the year following the tax year for which you are funding the IRA; e.g., your 1986 IRA must be opened and funded by April 15, 1987. Remember that an IRA is not an investment vehicle. It is, in effect, a retirement trust, and investments are managed for you in the IRA by a trustee or manager. A variety of vehicles are available in which to put your money for your IRA — ranging from conservative to relatively high risk. You can even have a self-directed IRA. Your investment advisers can help you with these investment strategies.

If you are self-employed and have an unincorporated business, there are pension plans fairly similar to corporate pension plans in which you can invest. Your banker, savings and loan representative, or broker can help you determine vehicles for the unincorporated retirement plan.

The corporation for which you work may offer plans to help you invest for retirement. Employee stock ownership plans (ESOPs), deferred compensation plans (401-k), and employee-sponsored IRAs known as qualified voluntary employee contribution plans (QVECs) are offered with tax advantages to employees. If your company offers such an opportunity, you should investigate the plan to determine if it has something to offer you. Talk with your investment advisers to decide if employer-offered plans can fit into your overall long-range financial planning.

If you have fifteen or more years until retirement, you will probably invest in such lower risk growth opportunities as selected stocks, mutual funds, and limited partnerships. If you have five to ten years before retirement, you will play it safer and accumulate money in government securities, insured certificates of deposit, safe bonds, and money market funds. It is important to make sure that you can get not only a return *on* your money but a return *of* your money the closer you are to retirement since your major earning years are nearing an end.

If you do not feel confident in investing for retirement under your own know-how, see a reputable financial planner who can create a plan for you based on your age, family responsibility, asset level, future needs, and the projected economy. Professional advice for retirement will be one of the greatest investments you can make in yourself and in your future.

PLE #9. AGING PARENTS

The fastest growing minority group in the United States is the group of people over age sixty-five. Growing old in such great numbers is a New Age phenomenon.[25] In the near future, it will not be uncommon to see three generations of one family all retired and taking care of one another. The White House Conference on Aging in 1981 reported that there are a greater number of people over age sixty-five in the United States than makes up the whole population of Canada. The over-sixty-five population of the world will swell to one billion strong by the year 2025 — equal to the present population of China.[26]

In a recent survey, it was found that most baby boomers took the Bible's commandment of "Honour thy father and mother" quite seriously. Three-quarters of the surveyed population felt a "great deal" of responsibility toward their aging parents.[27] It is a New Age reality that many parents will eventually become the responsibility of their children.

The best planning in caring for elderly parents comes from discussing with them how they want their affairs to be handled should they no longer be able to function due to mental or physical incapacity. Keeping the communication lines open while parents and children are well takes much of the emotion out of planning for the aging process.

You should have a list of your parents' professionals so that you can consult with them as it becomes necessary. If your parents trust you with the information, it is a good idea to know the location of all important papers and agreements and to have a list of all assets and liabilities. Even previous discussion of housing options and funeral arrangements can make such emotional occasions easier when they do occur. Your parents should execute the same planning for PLEs in life as you would, especially in the areas of disability and death planning discussed in this chapter.

One day you will be called upon to parent your parents, and that experience can be both painful and confusing. One of the saddest decisions children and parents are called upon to make is in the area of housing when the parents can no longer mentally and/or physically sustain themselves.

Many children share their home with their parents and find that it works out well—when finances are tight. However, sometimes it is not possible for generations to mix, and other living arrangements must be made. Local agencies on aging can be found in the telephone directory, and these organizations can help you to locate domestic services, meal provision, social services, day-care centers, and financial aid for the elderly.

If long-term care is necessary and finances permit, then you might consider nursing homes, adult day-care centers, life-care communities, and home health care. You should visit each facility for inspection before moving your parents. The American Association of Retired Persons (AARP) publishes *A Complete Guide To Long Term Care: National Continuing Directory* offering information on long-term care facilities in each state. That directory can be ordered from AARP, 1909 K Street NW, Washington, D.C. 20049.

Very few middle-income individuals can sustain their finances over a long period of time in a long-term institution. Statistics show that the average elderly person can pay for approximately a one-year stay in such an institution. After that time has elapsed, the individual must go on Medicaid or some other welfare program or be cared for by relatives. To qualify for Medicaid, the federal-state shared welfare program for the poor, an individual must use up essentially all his assets then sign over all Social Security payments. Some states are passing filial responsibility laws stating that children must also deplete their assets before the parent can receive Medicaid payments.

Little has been done concerning rising medical and custodial care costs for the elderly. This situation will be an area of major research and concern throughout the next fifteen years as the elderly population mushrooms. Some companies are offering nursing home insurance, but these programs are in their infancy.

At the present time, the best that you can do to care for your aging parent is:

1. Keep communication lines open. Discuss all options with them if possible. Treat them as you would want to be treated in the same situation.
2. Earn their trust. Give them no reason to distrust you.
3. Know as much about your parent's assets, liabilities, legal documents, insurance coverage, and other personal business as they feel comfortable in sharing with you.
4. Prepare to have some financial responsibility for parental care. Earmark 1–2% of your monthly savings for future care of your elderly parents.
5. Be familiar with all Medicare and Medicaid options. Deal in facts from the Social Security Administration not in hearsay or word of mouth from friends.

No amount of preliminary planning can totally relieve the painful experience you may have with your aging parents. However, financial planning can buy you more peace of mind and will purchase for your parents in old age more of the comfort they so richly deserve.

PLE #10. DEATH

Of all the PLEs, only death is certain. Although planning for your own death is less than pleasant, it will certainly be a favor to your family if you do.

At death your estate passes to your heirs or designated beneficiaries in such instruments as a will, employee benefits, IRA, and trusts. By seeking legal advice on estate planning, you can have proper instruments drawn for smoother passage of your estate and for transfer tax minimization if your estate is large enough to be taxed. The fees you pay for legal advice and financial planning in advance might save untold amounts of money for your family and other heirs.

The basis of an estate plan is a will. State laws control passage of your estate if you have no will. Some reasons for having such an instrument drafted are:

- You control who receives your property.
- There can be savings of death taxes and expenses through a properly drawn will.
- Estate settlement might hold fewer problems.
- Your estate will be managed as you wish because you appoint your manager (executor/executrix) in your will.[28]

It is also helpful to prearrange your funeral with a reputable funeral director. Be certain to see that money paid for pre-need arrangement is deposited to an account for you and not for the funeral director. Make sure your account will receive all income generated while the principal is being held. When you buy a cemetery plot, a deed is issued. Before making such a purchase, find out if there is an exchange privilege through a nationwide network should you choose to be buried in another town. Otherwise, you will be responsible for disposing of the plot yourself.

For family and tax planning purposes, many people set up trusts that are invoked after death by the will. Your trust officer, life insurance agent, lawyer, and financial planner can work together in advising you of the feasibility of such an instrument for your particular situation.

Make sure someone you trust knows the location of all your key papers and the value of all you own and owe. Survey the suggested steps to take after death, listed at the end of this chapter, to be sure that your executor would have all necessary information when you die.

Financial planning for death is also important. If you contribute to family income, you may need enough life insurance to supplement your family's income and to pay lump-sum expenses upon your death. A general guideline to use when purchasing life insurance is to purchase an amount equal to five to eight times your annual salary. If you are older and your family income is generated mostly from income-producing assets that you already own, you may not need so much insurance as when you were younger.

For those individuals with heavy death tax burdens, life insurance is often used to pay death taxes due within nine months

Prepare for Predictable Uncertainty 159

of death and payable in cash. Your financial planner and life insurance agent can help you in this area of planning.

When purchasing life insurance, consult *Best's Insurance Reports* for an A+ rated life insurance company. There are many life insurance companies, but there are a few who have a much better performance record than others. A. M. Best Company has a number of directories and journals that can help you to check out the best insurer for your life.

Another consideration in death planning is how you choose to take employee benefits and how your IRA is to be distributed. If you are married when you begin receiving benefits, you may choose to take a reduced amount over the lifetime of you and your spouse rather than having the benefits stop at your death. If you choose any other option, your spouse must approve and sign the paperwork.

With medical technology lengthening life, another consideration is how you wish to die. Many states have a Natural Death Act in their civil statutes. This document essentially says that you do not wish to be kept alive by artificial means or for heroic measures. That decision is totally up to you. This document, if legal in your state, may prevent some family anguish and conflict when you may not be in a position to make rational decisions.

If you wish to donate body organs to science or have various useful parts of your body used immediately for transplant, you can execute the proper paperwork through an attorney.[29] Often state driver's licenses allow you to designate disposition of various body parts.

You may not be the one to die. Often it is more difficult to lose someone close to you than it is to die yourself. If you are responsible for the estate of someone else, here are several steps to execute following that person's death. This list is not exhaustive, but it will be helpful in planning for the only certainty in life — death.

1. Check for donation of body parts if applicable. Execute proper procedures to carry out the decedent's wishes.
2. Contact the funeral director. Obtain the cemetery plot deed. Implement the decedent's instructions, if any. Funeral director will handle the details.
3. Proceed with notifying relatives, priest, rabbi, or minister, employer, friends, and business colleagues.
4. Notify lawyer and executor; locate the will. Do not try to

remove anything from safe deposit box without authorization.
5. Appoint someone to watch over the house of the deceased at all times during the time of death, funeral, burial, and immediate absence of the widow or widower.
6. Obtain eight to ten death certificates (more if necessary) as soon as possible. Funeral director normally handles this.
7. Arrange for a headstone to be placed at the grave, if applicable.
8. Meet with trustees if deceased had an *inter vivos* trust or other type of trust.
9. Notify life insurance agent of death, in order to start the paperwork and be ready to file when you present the agent with the death certificate. Check out even those policies that seem to be worthless. Select payment option.
10. Check for credit life insurance on debts or for other life insurance from fraternal organizations, credit card companies, societies, or credit unions. Go through check stubs for premium payments you may not know about.
11. Check for employee death benefits and execute the paperwork.
12. Apply for Social Security benefits, VA benefits, Civil Service benefits, Railroad Retirement benefits, or any other benefits.
13. Get credit cards and other charge accounts transferred if applicable. Cancel the deceased's cards.
14. Check for your medical insurance needs. If you are the spouse, you may be able to continue coverage. If you cannot, then you must apply for other benefits.
15. Change all insurance policies and benefits in which the deceased was named beneficiary.
16. Change partnership agreements, powers of attorney, or any other documents on which the deceased's name appeared.
17. You may possibly need to have a new will drafted for yourself if you are the spouse.
18. Cancel unnecessary magazine subscriptions.
19. Cancel and/or surrender all the decedent's identifications such as driver's license and passports.
20. Cancel fraternal organizations and unnecessary club memberships. Seek refunds if refunds will be available. Change memberships to another name if you wish to keep them.
21. The attorney will start probate procedure. You must work with the attorney on furnishing the proper information.
22. It must be determined whether or not IRS Form 706 (Transfer Tax) should be filed as well as state inheritance and/or estate tax forms. IRS Form 706 is due nine months

after date of death. Your state has its own rules for its forms. Your attorney, accountant, or trustee can fill out these forms for the executor.

23. Your executor can administer the estate by doing such things as changing titles, notifying insurance agents of needs for title change and coverage changes, inventorying and evaluating assets, paying debts, investing estate funds, managing or disposing of the business, paying taxes, and eventually distributing what is left over to the heirs.

In conclusion . . .

Sometimes unexpected guests arrive at my house for the weekend. If I have the guest rooms clean, the linens fresh and folded, and food in the refrigerator, I feel comfortable in having these people pop in. However, sometimes when surprise guests arrive, my house is in shambles, the wash has not been done for two weeks, and there is not even a morsel of bread in the cupboard. Then I panic! An unexpected event has happened for which I had not prepared.

Preparing for the PLEs is much like preparing for an unexpected guest. When proper planning is executed, stress is reduced and painful experiences are made easier. Without planning, panic sets in and events sometimes reach crisis proportions.

Remember, people do not plan to fail—they merely fail to plan.

NEW AGE FINANCIAL STRATEGIES

After proper planning for your PLEs with the appropriate financial professionals, you are ready to do surplus investing. Based on the predictability of uncertainty and emerging new rules, financial strategies for prosperity follow two basic ideas: (1) you must exercise individual responsibility for your own financial future; (2) you must diversify investments.

Here are some New Age financial guidelines to help you in your investment of your surplus. Please consider these only suggestions not advice. Before implementing *any* investment strategy, seek counsel from professionals. Never take suggestions from books literally until you and your advisers discuss how each situation affects you personally.

1. Change your thinking about money from a Second Wave attitude to a New Age attitude; i.e., from dependency to individual responsibility.

2. Diversification is a key to prosperity. Investments can be set up in order to take advantage of recession, depression, inflation, disinflation, and stable growth. Diversification for middle-income people can often be developed through mutual funds that meet your investment criteria.
3. Keep twelve months' expense equivalent in investments readily convertible to cash. Set this as a major goal to obtain by age forty.
4. By age fifty-five be able to generate at least 50% of lifestyle income from sources other than work.
5. By age sixty-five be able to totally live by income generated by sources other than work.
6. Begin your savings and investment program as soon as you begin to earn income. Invest a minimum of 10% of annual gross income; 20% of gross income is a great goal. Tighten your belt if necessary in order to meet this goal.
7. Consider your home a place to live instead of an investment.
8. Definitions of investments used later:

    Safe investments — those that are insured by the federal government directly, backed by the federal government directly, or insured by quasi-government bodies such as FDIC and FSLIC.

    Conservative investments — those that are either mutual funds or money market funds that invest in government backed investment securities, stable company stocks (blue chip), or real estate in multiple prime locations that are not overbuilt.

    Higher risk investments — those investments that are in growth-oriented companies that are taking a New Age power positioning philosophy, burgeoning industries with New Age technology and services, undeveloped real estate in areas projected for ten-to-twenty-year future growth, corporate bonds, and mutual funds investing in such instruments. Many tax-favored investments fit into this category.
9. Before age forty-five, seek higher risk growth opportunity with a majority of your investment money and place the remainder in conservative and safe investments.
10. Between ages forty-five and fifty-five seek growth opportunities with more of your investment funds in conservative investments, and less in higher risk growth opportunities and safe investments.
11. After age fifty-five, invest mostly in safe and conservative investments.[30]

Prepare for Predictable Uncertainty 163

Summary:

1. Because economics is a social science, it does not lend itself to a mathematical framework. It follows human experience.
2. Preparing to live with predictable uncertainty is a challenge at best. With the convulsive economy and global competition pressing our current economic structure, we must do the best we can to prepare for future situations.
3. Future events may reach crisis proportions unless preliminary planning takes place.
4. In the New Age, with predictable uncertainty a surety, security becomes a priority. Security is not only financially defined but is also a state of mind. Money offers financial security and buys freedom of choice and alleviation of many survival worries in life.
5. Financial prosperity in the New Age begins with a conversion of Second Wave money attitudes to New Age money attitudes.
6. Potential crises can be turned into Probable Life Events (PLEs). There are at least ten possible PLEs that you may be called on to face in the New Age:

   - Career interruption
   - Disability — physical, mental or legal through accidents, sickness or temporary detainment
   - Property loss
   - Liability lawsuit
   - Marriage/Remarriage
   - Children
   - Divorce
   - Retirement
   - Aging parents
   - Death

7. New Age financial investment strategies can be summarized as:

   - individual responsibility for future financial security, and
   - diversification.

Chapter 10

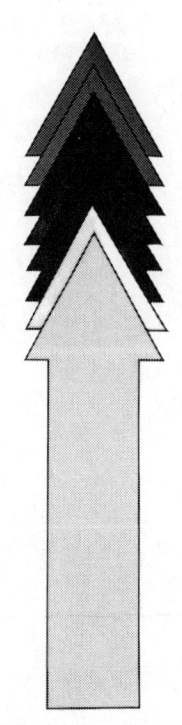

Release Yourself To Relate

Friendship, after all, is what life is finally about. Everything material and professional exists in the end for persons.
— Nels F. S. Ferre

The Second Wave Economy fostered materialistic concerns that played havoc with psychological comfort. Foremost in the minds of business people and politicians during the Second Wave were production, consumption, bottom line, and competition.

In power positioning for the New Age, however, the great determinant of your success will be your power with people. The New Age breeds strength through sharing, relationship development, pooling, and human capital. Technological innovation of the Second Wave released us from many of the *physical* chores. Technological innovation of the New Age will release us from many of our *intellectual* chores. Therefore, with many physical and cognitive activities conducted for us by technology, we will have more time and energy to relate to people. Computers and robots may replace many of the processes of the human being, but they will never replace humanness.

Even in an age of high technology, people skills are more important than ever before. The Carnegie Institute of Technology has found that, even in such fields as engineering, 15% of one's financial success can be attributed to technical knowledge; whereas, 85% of financial success comes from an individual's people skills.[1]

The ability to make and maintain relationships during the New Age will be of prime importance. When you have a relationship, you have "mutual empathy" with another person; i.e., each of you will understand the other and can imagine yourself in the other's place. You will then act and react accordingly. No matter what role you play, relationship development is a key issue. The ability to manage sound relationships is important to leadership development. According to Bill Lareau, a Kentucky organizational consultant and author, potential leaders often emerge from unexpected personality traits. Leadership is not so much the asserting of one personality on a group as it is the tailoring of your particular personality style from a repertoire of skills to meet particular needs in people, according to the Research Institute of America.[2] Therefore, in management and leadership positions, the people who have the best range of skills to meet individual needs are those people who become the better leaders.

Selling also requires relationship development. The area of sales will change as the economy becomes more service and technology oriented according to the *Harvard Business Review*. "The ongoing nature of services and the growing complexity of technology will increasingly necessitate lengthy and involved relationships between buyers and sellers. Managing relationships within the dynamics of the sales process will be much like managing relationships between husbands and wives," says Theodore Levitt, the Edward W. Carter professor of business administration of Harvard Business School.[3] Repeat orders will go to those sales people who have the greatest ability to nurture long-term relationships.

In 1982, the Canadian Conference of Catholic Bishops released a report condemning corporations and governments for placing greater importance on profits than people. Bishops called for an emphasis on human needs and a de-emphasis on maximization of profits and growth. In his book, *The Poverty of Affluence*, Paul Wachtel underscores the concerns of the bishops. Wachtel argues that in America there is a standard of living far superior to any other the world has ever known, yet more people are feeling psychologically deprived than ever before.[4] The Second Wave commitment to growth, productivity, and consumption resulted in people's defining their lives according to the things they could accumulate, and they began to identify self-worth with accumulation of money as a way to keep score. With materialism a primary concern, the American people in the Second Wave sacrificed intimacy, family life, and friendship.

Although money offers freedom of choice and is a contributor to peace of mind in the New Age, the intensive pursuit of consumption, thereby putting yourself in bondage financially, will produce psychological discomfort. Healthy relationship development which emphasizes spiritual mutuality will fulfill much of the deprivation that Second Wave America felt in the intense pursuit of materialism.

Whether you are seeking financial well-being, leadership success, or personal gratification in the New Age, your talent and skill in relationship management will be a tremendous determinant to your peace of mind. In Chapter 8, we discussed resource connectors, i.e., people who can help you to get what you want from life as well as meet many of your psychological needs. This chapter deals with how we can invest in relationships in order to reap psychological rewards. It is not enough simply to find other people to meet your needs as resource connectors; you must also learn how to contribute to the needs of other people. Relationship development is two-way. You have a primary responsibility in the discovery and significance of each relationship in your life.

Relationships are like any other commodity. You can carelessly spend them or you can invest in them for maximum return and rewards. By creatively investing in relationships, you seal a bond resulting in a spiritual condition known as "like" or "love." Relationship development begins with your attitude, is enhanced through communication, and is solidified through specific action. In order to I-N-V-E-S-T in relationships, there are six essential ingredients:

I – represents the respect of **individualism**
N – stands for complementary **needs**
V – represents **values** synchronization
E – is for **empathy**
S – indicates the development of **self-esteem** in the other person
T – represents **trust** in the relationship.[5]

A discussion of each of these entities of relationships follows.

INDIVIDUALISM

Relationship development begins with respect for the other person's individualism. As we have mentioned so many times throughout this book, each person on earth is a unique organism and cannot be duplicated. So often, however, in relationships we tend to feel that other people should be like we are. They should have similar traits, habits, and characteristics. If they do not, then we consider them abnormal, weird, or strange. However, the opposite is true. In entering a relationship, you first develop the attitude that everybody is different. Each person has a unique contribution to make. It is up to us to find those talents and abilities in that other person so that we can respect those traits. Look for the good in the other person because every person has good points. Avoid looking for negative traits, habits, and characteristics. You will find what you expect.

In developing an attitude of respect for other people's individualism, you first must release your "self" to relate. If in communication, conversation, or relationship development you continually think of yourself, then your mind cannot be on the other person. You cannot be concentrating on the essentials of relationship development. Think of the contributions you can make to the relationship as opposed to what this person can give to you in the potential relationship. Forget yourself and make the other person a priority. It takes a tremendous amount of ego strength and maturity to feed the other individual's ego needs. Very few people have attained the state of mind that will allow them to release the "self" or ego to concentrate on the other person's "self" or ego.

Though each person with whom you come in contact will be unique, there will be personality trends that will be predictable. When you learn to recognize these personal behavior styles through listening, observation, and questioning, you will become an instant expert in human relations. Although there are many styles of behavior, these characteristics can be boiled down into four primary profiles.

The first behavior profile is the **ORGANIZER**. People with this profile respond to an orderly, systematic approach. They like organized people, and they are very organized themselves. Their office and home are normally very neat with everything in place. In their work environment, they have on their desks only those papers on which they are working. The remainder of any paperwork will be on a credenza or filed away in the appropriate place. The walls of their home or office will be neatly arranged. In the office environment, the walls will contain evidence of credibility because one of the major objectives of the organizer is to be correct. It is important to them to be right. In fact, if they could carve anything on their tombstone before they die, they would engrave, "I was right."

Before making any decision, organizers must know all the facts. Decision making is difficult for organizers because any time a decision is to be made, there is a risk of being wrong; and organizers emphasize correctness or rightness. They are very detailed both in speech patterns, explanation, and in writing. If you work for such an individual, that person will expect very detailed reports from you. They expect you to do your homework. In fact, organizers rarely give you a second chance to create a good first impression. If organizers determine you are not detailed and you have not done your homework adequately, it will be very difficult to get back into their good graces again.

Because decision making is difficult for them, organizers do not make quick decisions. It is important to set up goals, directions, and deadlines for organizers because they will get so bogged down in data analysis that they may fail to meet deadlines and goals unless they are previously set. They do not like to impose ideas on others until they are certain of the outcome. Organizers do not function well in an environment where information is scant or incomplete. For instance, if they are put into a sales environment where training is inadequate and they do not feel that their knowledge of the product line is complete, then they will not have confidence in approaching the prospect. Organizers are very good listeners. Their philosophy is that we were given two ears and one mouth and those body parts are to be used in those proportions. Listening is another way of gathering data, and data gathering is of primary emphasis to the organizer.

When presenting ideas or proposals, it is good to give organizers choices because they like to arrive at their own decisions. Organizers do not like to be told what to think or how to think.

Safety, peace of mind, and stability are very important priorities. A person who is a dominant organizer profile likes to work with data and things rather than people. If organizers are in a career that has a high level of people contact, they will be under more stress than when working with machines or manipulating data.

A second type of behavior style is the COMPETITOR profile. Competitors are movers and shakers. They move to production very quickly and are tremendously goal-oriented. Of any of the personality types described, these individuals are the most end-result-oriented. If anyone or anything gets in the way of their target, competitors will quickly move the obstacle aside and be on the way to their goal.

Competitors are not detailed persons. When presented with ideas, they appreciate a capsular approach. Detail bores them. Competitors enjoy doing things their own way. In fact, competitors are very poor listeners because they spend a great deal of time telling people what to do as opposed to gathering data and listening for ideas and alternatives. Competitors like to make the rules and expect their rules to be followed. If this type of individual is a subordinate, he appreciates work assignments that allow total freedom. Competitors do not like to be watched after an assignment has been made. They like to receive instructions for a task, go away, and then bring the results back on the due date assigned.

Competitors have been credited with hurting people's feelings. Because of the fast-moving, goal-directed, take-charge behavior style, sometimes competitors are not as sensitive to other people's feelings as some of the other personality styles discussed. If competitors are expected to be counselors or to work in any kind of an environment that requires nurturing and listening, they will not function well. They like to win and would carve on their tombstones, "I won."

Competitors are very high risk. They are gamblers and may win and lose several fortunes in a lifetime. They enjoy the task itself and like to quantify results in the form of money, point system, or bonus activity.

Because this particular personality profile is very competitive, they treat the world with finite value. In other words, competitors, if in a sales contest, feel that there is a finite amount of success to be had, and if they do not win, someone else will reap the reward. Competitors find it very difficult to share or to pool information for success. They view the world as a win/lose situation.

The competitor's office or home environment evidences a fast-moving, time-conscious individual. There will be many conveniences for time-savings in both the home and the office. Competitors will probably have a telephone in the car. Convenience is a necessity. They do not appear nearly so organized as the organizer. You might find piles of paperwork in neat stacks. The walls of the office and home are normally decorated with appropriate artwork as well as trophies to denote the victor's spoils. The speech pattern of the competitor is rapid fire. Ordinarily, the first few words of the sentence are slower than the last three words of the sentence. The longer the competitor talks, the faster the speech pattern becomes.

The third personality profile is the ENTERTAINER. This individual is very eager to please other people. In fact, entertainers are very people-oriented. Tasks, data, things, and machines are not rewarding nor motivating to them. They get their ego strength and major rewards in life from being praised and recognized by other people. In fact, entertainers become very depressed when taken out of a people-contact environment. They like exciting, fast-moving, inspirational activities and are not very concerned with detail. Entertainers, if assigned a task involving much detail, may have many errors. If an entertainer is your subordinate, check the person's detail for accuracy.

After giving instructions to entertainers, it is important to ask for and assess feedback from them. Entertainers' minds tend to wander while they are being given instructions because they are interested in so many diverse activities that it is hard for them to concentrate for much more than a fifteen-minute period of time.

It is easy for entertainers to get off track in conversation and in goal-directed activity. Entertainers find it very difficult to exercise self-discipline because their interests lie in so many diverse areas in work and in life. Entertainers are not exacting individuals, but generalizing individuals. It is difficult for entertainers to pinpoint time.

For example, if you set up an 11 A.M. appointment with an entertainer, this person may be half an hour to an hour late because organization is not a priority nor is time management. Entertainers like people and like to be admired by people. They like to perform in front of a crowd. They are not necessarily professional performers, but at social gatherings, in the office, or at home they will be the "life of the party." Entertainers especially emphasize status, prestige, and social recognition.

The office and home environment of the entertainer is very colorful. You might even find inspirational plaques posted on the walls. Entertainers are very contemporary in their decor and in their personal image. Their speech pattern is very voice-inflected. You can detect excitement or sadness or any of the various moods through which entertainers go, simply by listening very carefully to their voice patterns. They are very animated when they speak. Their moods are easily detectable, and they have a variety of moods.

If entertainers could carve anything on their tombstones, they would put, "Everybody admired me." This profile is a very high-risk person. Most of the risks the entertainer takes come from the risks in relationships rather than risks in business ventures. Of all four personality styles, the entertainer is the most other-directed. Their confidence and self-esteem are directly correlated to their perception of what other people think of them.

The fourth personality style is the RELATER. This profile likes to please others. If relaters could carve an inscription on their tombstones, they would say, "Everybody liked me." This statement is different from the entertainer because the entertainer likes to be admired from afar and does not like for people to get too close to them; relaters like intimate one-on-one relationships. They will allow people to see their vulnerabilities.

Relaters need a specific track to follow. They find it difficult to be totally goal-directed because relaters are constantly resetting priorities. Relationships are of top priority to them. If anyone gets in trouble or expresses a need for the relater's time and friendship, then relaters will respond to that need even if they are on their way to a goal. This individual is highly safety-oriented. Security, guarantees, and safety are emphasized in relationships. Relaters are extremely loyal and form friendships for a lifetime. If friends or acquaintances move to other areas, and the relater is in the area on a business or social trip, then the relater will stop by for a visit. People are very important to the relater.

Relaters enjoy being members of a team. They respect loyalty. They need praise and follow-up from family, friends, and co-workers. Relaters do not like bossy people. When asking them to perform a task or giving a work assignment, it is helpful for them to have input and to be able to think of the project from a team point-of-view as opposed to a we-they point-of-view as in management versus subordinates.

Relaters are very friendly, and their major goal is to be liked above all else. Relaters do not enjoy conflict and will steer clear of those particular situations if at all possible. This personality type will put others before their own goals. The relater is a very giving, charitable individual. In fact, relaters sometimes allow themselves to be used by other people. Because they are very nurturing, helpful, loyal, and kind, they spend most of their lives helping other people to get where they want to go.

The office or home environment of the relater is very warm. You will find brown tones, gentle colors, green plants, and a warm fireplace burning in the winter. The "number one" objective of the relater is to make people feel comfortable on the relater's home turf. Their attitude is for relationships to be "win-win." Relaters are tremendous listeners and are concerned about hearing from you as opposed to talking about themselves. Their speech pattern will be somewhat slow, calm, warm, but with not too much animation or emotion. Many of the detailed, organized traits of the relater are similar to those of the organizer. The relater expresses much warmth and genuine caring but is not as emotional as the entertainer.

Relaters are inner-directed and are very at peace when they feel that they have done something to benefit humanity.

Now that we have reviewed these four personality types, let me emphasize that there is no good, bad, better, or worse personality style. Each style has its own unique traits, habits, and characteristics. Each of these profiles has strengths and each has weaknesses. In fact, strengths taken to excess become weaknesses in each of these styles. It is important to recognize and respect the person's individual differences. When relating to people, after you have decided which type they are, you can then relate to them by giving them what you feel they want as opposed to giving them what you want them to have. This particular attitude is a real secret to successful relationship development. When we give other people what they want as opposed to what we feel we want them to have, we operate in their relational territory rather than asking them to come into ours.

Last Christmas, an artist friend of mine designed hand-painted shirts for four of my special friends. Knowing what each of these individuals liked, we conceptualized artwork on each garment that we felt each individual would enjoy. Upon watching their excitement as they opened their gifts, we knew that we had pleased each person. My artist friend commented: "You know, I was afraid one particular friend would not like her shirt because I personally did not favor the design. But after watching her excitement over the artwork, I realized that designing what she liked rather than what I liked was important."

This experience with the specifically designed shirts as gifts holds a great lesson. Even though we may feel that people are different from us, when we communicate with them and relate to them based on their wants, needs, and desires, we can then create a solid relationship. When we expect them to relate to us based on our needs, desires, and expectations, those relationships are not as solid and may completely fail.

In appealing to a person's individualism, there are specific power phrases you can use. Such phrases as:

- "What do you think?"
- "How do you feel about this?"
- "If you were me, what would you do?"

These phrases cause the individual to know that you respect them and where they are coming from as opposed to expecting them to meet you where you are. Communicating with these phrases in developing relationships will help the other person to know that you respect their individualism.

NEEDS

Another ingredient in maintaining relationships is to seek the needs of another person and go about fulfilling those needs. You must first make the assumption that everybody has needs. I know that you see some people in life who seemingly do not need anything from you, but you must realize that everybody has a need. They have something about themselves that they would change if they could. There is dissatisfaction in everybody's life, and everyone is seeking fulfillment. No one is totally 100% happy.

There are several common needs that are true for all individuals. In developing relationships, you can start with these particular needs.

1. *Another person needs the investment of your time.* Relationships cannot be developed without time being spent on the process. Dr. James Pleitz, pastor of Park Cities Baptist Church in Dallas, says that love is spelled "T-I-M-E." You can verbally commit to someone that you care for them; yet if you never seem to have time for them, the message that they get from you is that you really do not care. *What you say verbally is not nearly so important as what you do through your actions.* Spending time — quality, constructive time with another individual sharing, communicating, doing things you both enjoy — is an expression from you that the other person holds high priority in your life. If you've noticed, you always have time for those things that are important to you.

Several weeks ago in a counseling session, a young man told me that he did not believe that his mother ever loved him. I asked him why he felt that way, and he said, "Because she never had time for me. She always seemed to be working or going to social activities or engaged in civic work. I always seemed to come last." Even though in her heart the mother may have put her son first, in her actions and in his perceptions, the son was last on the priority list. Today, the young man feels deprived of love and affection. He is having difficulty with his own self-esteem and in accepting himself.

Time commitment is not only an expression between parents and children, but it is also an expression of interest and caring on the part of management. On one consulting assignment in a corporation, I heard an employee say, "I never can seem to find my manager in the office. I don't guess she cares for me. Every time I ask if I can talk with her about something, she asks if it can wait until later. She never seems to have time for me. She never seems to care." As managers and leaders in organizations, it is important to give your time and to listen to your subordinates. Today, corporations are crying for employee loyalty and for better productivity and performance. A seemingly little thing — such as giving your time to your employees to show interest in them personally — can cause a big difference in the quality of their work and their interest in organizational goals. You can never expect a person to be interested in you until you first show that you are interested in them.

2. *A second need of most people is the need to be needed.* Even though there is risk involved, dare to be vulnerable in front of the person with whom you wish to establish a relationship. Everyone needs to feel that someone else needs them. That situation puts them in a power position and automatically elevates their feelings of strength. In cases like this, even the weak become strong. It has been said that a person's need to love is perhaps greater than an individual's need to be loved.

A friend of mine has recently lost her husband. Her children are adults and do not live near her. However, one of her grandchildren became very ill last month, and the recently widowed grandmother went to help her daughter care for the sick child. I called the daughter's home early last week to check on the health status of the child, and the grandmother answered the telephone. She informed me that the child was doing very well and that she would be back to full health very soon. But the grandmother said to me, "You know, I would not have wished this ill health on my grandchild for anything in the world. But for me it has almost been a blessing in disguise because for the first time since my husband died I feel needed." There are many lonely people in the world — young, middle-aged, and elderly. *And this loneliness stems* not so much from the fact that these people feel that no one cares for them, but that there is no one for whom to care.

Therefore, if you have a basic flaw that you can share with an individual whom you trust or if you have a real need which you feel they can fulfill, then share these thoughts with that person. In the work environment, asking a subordinate to help develop ideas or for input on a project makes that subordinate feel important and a part of the overall organization. The time that you spend soliciting opinions from your subordinates is time well invested in the growth of your organization.

People need to feel needed. Relationships will be solidified through sharing and fulfilling of mutual needs.

3. *A third need that most people have is the need for touch.* There are times and places to physically touch someone. Normally, the work environment allows no more than a handshake, which is the common form of comradeship, friendliness, and greeting in the business world. But there are other forms of touch that are appropriate to business. One type of touch is warmth in your voice. Rather than being aggressive and threatening to other individuals, you can be calm, warm and genuinely concerned through tone of voice. This substitutes for the physical touch.

However, in personal life, touch is very important. It is important between husband and wife, parents and children, and even among friends. The skin is the most sensitive part of your body housing millions of sensory fibers. Often a person can function by losing many of the senses — sight, hearing, smell, taste — but it becomes literally impossible to survive without being touched and stimulated. The need for contact is important not only in human beings but also in animals. Dogs and cats like to be stroked and petted. Many animals lick their newborn. Psychologist Harry Harlow has found that there is a strong need for contact with a mother or a mother figure among baby monkeys.[6] Researchers Weininger, McClellan, and Arima have found that rats that were handled and petted for ten minutes per day for a three-week period after they were weaned grew bigger, better, and had less fear than a control group of comparable rats.[7] Montagu studied the death rate in infants in orphanages and found that there was a much higher death rate among those infants not held close to someone for at least a few minutes per day. He further suggested that such contact comfort as kissing, holding hands, touching, rubbing noses, handshaking, and stroking of the hand are simply means of fulfilling a need for touch in people's lives.[8]

People long to be touched. In the business world this can be done by the demonstration of a handshake, leaning forward while someone is talking with you, eye contact to show intensive listening, a gentle touch of the shoulder, slap on the back, or with a gentle handshake with the left hand coming down over the total handshake and enclosing it.

As a warning to touching in the business world, the caveat is: if in doubt, do not touch other than by handshake on first meeting someone. The touching, relationship building, and needs development in business come only after you feel confident that you know the person well.

Remember, the first impression is very important. In the business world, we want to appear very professional. A formal handshake may possibly be the only form of physical touching you will ever use. Though you may become less formal as professional relationships grow, it is always in good taste to use discretion when choosing how and when to touch.

Male and female should be very aware of the amount of touching that goes on in the office environment so that these gestures will not be misconstrued among business associates.

Conversational power phrases to use in fulfilling one's universal needs are:

- "Will you help me?"
- "I need you. Do you have a second?"
- "I need your input."

Touching, investment of time, and sharing vulnerability are all universal needs of the human being. In developing relationships in the New Age, it is so important that other people know that we recognize their humanness.

VALUES SYNCHRONIZATION

A third foundation upon which relationships are built is common values. We tend to like people who have much in common with us. The opposite situation also holds true. Other people like us if we hold a lot in common with them. A real relationship builder in talking with someone is the use of the words, "Me, too." If you look hard enough and long enough, you can find values in another person that can be synchronized with your own values. This may take a series of questions and intensive listening, but it can be done.

In synchronizing values, it is important to ask non-threatening questions. Basically, the values you have in common will probably

Release Yourself to Relate 177

be in the areas of education, the place where you grew up, hobbies, work values, or philosophy. In order to question people about these areas, you should ask general questions and ask them very tactfully. Here are some examples.

1. To find out about a person's family ask them: "Are you a family person?" That particular question leaves the person open to answer you in one of several ways. Be careful not to say:
    - "Are you single?"
    - "Are you married?"
    - "Why don't you have children?"

    These questions tend to threaten the other person and could perhaps put their ego on the defensive. But asking the open-ended question will allow the person to expand and explain in any direction he or she wishes.
2. Another helpful question is: "How did you choose your career?" This question, again, is open-ended and allows that person to elaborate. This will help you get to know the individual's motives, likes, and dislikes. It opens up inner feelings. Your responsibility is to listen for clues whereby you may synchronize values.
3. A third appropriate question for getting to know another person is: "Are you from this area?" This question allows the person to tell you about his or her childhood, developmental stages, and places where he lived. By knowing this information, you will have clues to cultural values, philosophies, and attitudes toward life.

There are other general questions which are appropriate in getting to know another's value systems. You should remember to ask non-threatening, open-ended questions that allow people to reveal themselves as they wish rather than forcing them to defend their egos and self-esteem.

Participatory management is a way to synchronize values in the business world. By getting workers involved in the management process, they help make the decisions and, therefore, feel obligated to carry out those decisions even if many long hours are involved in accomplishing those goals. Corning Glassworks in Corning, New York, began a participatory management program in 1984. In one situation, a die manufacturing problem needed to be solved. Five machinists were formed into a committee and were put in a room to solve the problem. All the information and necessary tools were provided for them. After approximately five hours, the team had solved the manufacturing problem with a cost of less than

$200. At that time, the team was synchronizing values and working toward a common goal.

Such companies as Eggers Industries and TRW, Inc. are emphasizing people skills in the management process. They have gone so far as to reassign first-line supervisors and managers to jobs that did not involve the supervision of workers if these people could not demonstrate viable people skills and flexibility in management style. If these managers could not promote participatory management and could not adapt to the New Age management process, they were replaced in their positions.[9] The ability to manage teams and to make teams productive in the New Age will rely heavily on management talents in promoting commonalities among people. The secret is to cause people to pull together rather than apart. Not only will the success of your particular career depend on it, but the success of your company as well.

Power phrases to use in the solicitation of value synchronization are:

- "Can you help me?"
- "What do you think about this?"
- "Do you have any ideas for improvement?"
- "How can we save money?"

Your ability to build on common values is a great contributory factor in relationship maintenance. The more you and another person share in common, the deeper your relationship will be.

EMPATHY

When you project yourself into another person's position or situation through your imagination, you are exercising empathy. And greater empathy in relationships is enhanced through communication. Most people think they are communicating when in actuality they are just giving instructions or merely talking. No communication has actually taken place until mutual understanding has been achieved.

In the New Age, with service and people skills at a premium, your ability to have empathy for the sake of communication and relationship building is invaluable. Organizational consultants have indicated that 75% of verbal communication is misunderstood. Therefore, mutual understanding is accomplished only 25% of the time — which leaves much room for growth and improvement.

Release Yourself to Relate

Several physicians have found that, in at least 90% of the cases, diagnosis is made by listening to the patient. It stands to reason that listening is a great part of the communication process. Sometimes we hear, but we are not listening.

Ethel M., a middle-aged friend of mine, telephoned me the other day and was quite upset. She said that she had gone to the doctor, and he had run a series of tests on her. Just before she telephoned me, the nurse had called her to tell her that the doctor wanted her to come in on the following Monday for an *autopsy*. Then she started to cry. Through her tears she said, "You know medical technology has come a long way, hasn't it? You used to have to be dead to do that." Sitting there with the telephone receiver in my hand, my words stuck in my throat. There was no way Ethel could go in on Monday for an autopsy. Modern technology has improved our lives a great deal, but Ethel still had to be dead to have an autopsy performed. After thinking a moment, I responded: "Ethel, do you feel that the nurse may have said for you to come into the office for a biopsy?" Ethel stopped crying, and I could hear the relief in her voice as she said, "Yes, I bet that's what she said."

Ethel had been quite upset not by what she heard but by what she thought she heard. Perhaps there had been a barrier to her listening when she was speaking with the nurse. In fact, often there are barriers to effective listening. Some of these barriers are:

- being so emotionally involved in a statement that the statement is misinterpreted
- having a negative attitude toward the one who is speaking
- being hurried and not having your mind on the conversation
- being confused by the statement but being unwilling to ask the speaker for clarification
- communicating at the improper time or in the wrong place
- intentionally not listening while thinking about something else
- such handicaps as hearing or sight to decrease observation
- inability or unwillingness to give proper feedback, and
- being fatigued while communicating.

For effective listening to take place, it is essential to remove all possible barriers.

Here are ten suggestions for the improvement of listening skills.

1. Have an intense desire to listen.

2. Let the other person know that you are aware of his or her presence and that you really want to hear what he or she has to say.
3. Remove any barriers or distractions to your effective listening.
4. Listen with intense interest, and respond only at specific times with effective feedback.
5. Be an objective listener. Do not argue or criticize the speaker either mentally or in actuality. Your goal is understanding, not triumph.
6. Be patient while listening. Leave ample time for the other person to finish verbal communication.
7. Repeat statements back to the speaker. If you do not understand what the speaker is saying, ask for clarification. Ask questions to show interest during the verbal communication of the speaker.
8. Look for the theme and the main points of the message the speaker is trying to get across to you. Often the speaker does not stick to the point. Make an effort to find the point and to stick to it yourself.
9. Use your observation skills — both ears and eyes — to listen for voice inflection, pauses, emotion, tones, facial expression, and other body language.
10. Do not interrupt the speaker with anything but feedback pertaining to the conversation. Do not interrupt the conversation process and get off on a tangent talking about additional information, other subjects, or yourself.

In addition to listening with your ears, you listen through your eyes via observation. The first thing you notice about people are their clothes, which tell you a great deal about how they view themselves. If they are ill-groomed, then they normally have lower self-esteem than those people who are well-groomed. The second feature that you notice is one's face. The overall features indicate such states of mind as happiness, peace, hostility, or depression. Such specific features as eyebrows, area between the eyebrows, eyes, and mouth can be read for specific information.

For example, a hollowed look from the eyes and a smile from one side of the mouth accompanied by a slight knit of the eyebrows can denote that the other person is not exercising total disclosure or honesty with you. Body position, tightness of muscles, and placement of the hands can indicate whether a person is comfortable in your presence. The observing of behavior and body language is an interesting topic, but extensive discussion of it is beyond the scope of this chapter.

The ability to say what you mean in a tone correlated with that meaning takes real talent. Many people talk but do not communicate with effective verbal behavior. As a sender of communication messages, you have a responsibility to remove as many barriers as possible. Such barriers to the speaker are

- being hurried and not forming your words properly or talking too rapidly
- improper attitude toward your listener or toward what you are telling the person
- the message that you are sending is unclear to you; i.e., you do not understand what you are saying
- poor communicating skills
- wrong time or improper place
- not asking for feedback from the listener
- no empathy for your listener, and
- unmeaningful messages to the listener.

Each message you convey should have a central theme or main point, and you should stick to that main point without confusing the listener with superfluous information. The message should be clear, concise, appropriate, and meaningful. It is important to keep the favorable attention of the listener throughout the process.

Simple verbal communication and listening are not as meaningful without involvement of the listener in the total communication. The average adult attention span is approximately 1.9 minutes before the mind begins to wander. If the listener is actively involved in the process, then more learning, persuasion, and understanding takes place. From merely hearing, the listener remembers only 20% of what is said. But through involvement, the listener will retain 90% of what is said. Various avenues that you can take to involve the listener in communication are:

Involvement:	You can have a listener take notes, write down figures, give feedback, or make a list.
Association:	You can tell stories of other people into which the listener can project his/her own situation. The listener can associate things in his life with the characters in your stories. This is much the same effect as when a person gets involved in a movie.
Demonstration:	You can use props in your demonstration or even use pictures, movies, or slide presentations. If you are demonstrating how a finished

Motivation: report should look, you can draw the finished product for your listener. The purpose is to cause the listener to become mentally or physically involved.

Motivation: Knowing what causes a person to get excited and to want to perform helps in communication. The entertainer is motivated by inspirational stories. The organizer is motivated by receiving ample, objective information. The competitor is motivated by being able to put him/herself in a situation where he/she can win. The relater is motivated by the capability of being helpful. Of the various power phrases cited throughout this chapter, decide which will be motivating to your listener — depending on the goal you are trying to accomplish.

Questions: Ask the listener questions as you are speaking. Allow time for a response and really listen to the answers. Let the speaker know that communication is two-way.

Emotion: The entertainer and relater respond to emotion better than the organizer and competitor. The one whom emotion least affects is the organizer. However, in working with each style, if you know what is meaningful to each one, you can tell stories and relate to events or even people in each individual's life that will bring an emotional response from them. People remember what emotionally affects them. The message, then, carries much greater meaning and is retained better when there is emotional involvement.[10]

These suggestions were presented in Northwestern Mutual Life Insurance Company Career School of 1979. They are techniques often used to involve the buyer in the sales process. However, each time you send a message through communication, i.e., each time you speak, you are really selling your listener on something. Therefore, these techniques work in any communication process — not just in sales. You can apply empathic communication with the personal styles of people described earlier in the chapter. When you determine a person's basic style, you can communicate in a way that is important to that person and not to you. You would communicate with the organizer in detail — maybe even presenting the pros and cons of your ideas. The competitor would respond to you well if you kept your message short and in summary, bottom-line format. With the relater you would allow time to build a relationship and learn personal facts before communicating about business. The entertainer expects lively, animated, inspirational communication. You would not wish to share information with the entertainer when you are either in a bad mood or slightly depressed.

Communication takes place on three levels: surface, intellectual, and feeling. Often when we first meet someone, we communicate on surface level. The discussion of the weather, specific facts, and non-threatening information is exchanged. When you get to know a person better, you begin to communicate on the intellectual level. Information is exchanged in a logical, adult manner. Still, however, the third level has not been reached. When you develop a really lasting, strong relationship, you are capable of communicating on the feeling level. In this step, information is exchanged about your innermost fears, joys, anxieties, and sadnesses. When a relationship is built on the feelings level, time seems to fly rapidly as you share those feelings. Often during the love bonding process — either through development of friendship or in pre-approach to-marriage — the feeling level is exchanged readily. However, as relationships wane, people return to the surface or intellectual levels of conversation. The depth of a relationship can be determined by the level at which two people communicate.

Power phrases to express empathy are:

- "I understand."
- "I know how you feel."
- "Tell me more . . . "

SELF-ESTEEM

The greatest need of all humans is to feel unique and important. Perhaps this need is never totally satisfied. In building self-esteem, one needs to feel loved, appreciated, recognized, rewarded, encouraged, and worthy. The greater you contribute to this ego need in the other person, the more solid your relationship will be.

Sometimes you will meet a person who seems to need no self-esteem building. In fact, you feel that if you compliment him, you will create a monster. All he does is compliment himself and his achievements. Do not be misled. He is feeding his ego because he has needs which are not being fulfilled by other people. Rather than avoid building that person's self-esteem, do the opposite. Work on his ego all the more. He will like you for reaffirming his greatest need — to hear someone verbalize approval. Remember, one only talks about food when one is hungry. By the same token, one compliments self only when the ego is hungry for affirmation.

Here are seven ideas for building self-esteem in other people.

1. Motivate the other person. Tell them what they do well. Encourage them in their tasks and activities. Always seem to be the person who is there to help.
2. Give away your material wealth to people. Buy gifts — especially gifts that you know will be meaningful to the other person. The presentation of gifts indicates that you care enough to invest your time and money — both very precious resources in the New Age — to make that other person happy.
3. Make people feel important by listening to them and exercising the good listening skills discussed earlier in this chapter. When you hear the other person allude to an accomplishment, even though you may wish to top that accomplishment, do not. Your pride may want to say in some subtle way:"Well, I can tell you one better than that . . . " You may boost your own ego, but, you will deflate the other person's. For example, John and his friend Jim both enjoy being in the public eye. They do much civic work and their names are in the newspapers several times per year. Because they empathize with each other's need to feel important, they exchange newspaper clippings about themselves. Each understands that the other likes to be called and congratulated when a newspaper clipping is received. One day John received a newspaper clipping from Jim about a civic award that Jim had just received. Coincidentally, John had just written Jim a letter and enclosed three articles that had recently appeared about him. John never mailed those articles. Because of his respect for Jim and not wanting to steal the glory of Jim's moment, John withheld his articles so that Jim could feel important at this time. That is a relationship-building skill. That is putting another person's ego above one's self.
4. Compliment specifics about a person. Instead of telling one that he is handsome, tell that person what beautiful hair he has or how nice he looks in a particular suit. People enjoy knowing why you are saying complimentary things about them. The greatest gift that you can give someone is a compliment. The next greatest gift that you can give someone is to pass on a compliment that you have heard about

the person. Many people withhold telling others good things that they have heard about them because they do not want the person to get the "big head." However, when you pass on compliments, the opposite effect normally takes place. The other person becomes endeared to you and even more humbled because you shared that information with them.

5. When you read about another person in the newspaper or hear that they have gotten a promotion or have achieved anything of significance, write that person a note, send a card, or telephone the individual. Often we hesitate to recognize achievements because we feel that the person is receiving so much recognition that our phone call or note would not even be noticed. Most people are in such need of recognition that all notes, cards, and phone calls are noticed and are totally appreciated. Another form of recognition is to give people proper credit for work done. If you are in management or if one of your peers had a good idea, always give that individual credit for the idea or for the accomplishment of the work. Public recognition is even more effective than private recognition. If you can compliment someone's achievement in front of another person, it will mean more than if you compliment that person in private. Organizational studies show that one's performance increases when he is praised in public as opposed to when the manager simply praises performance in private.

6. Compliment and affirm the things and people with whom that person is associated. For instance, if an individual's child has a significant achievement, compliment that person's child. Things that are meaningful to the individual, when affirmed, will mean the same as if you are complimenting that person. For example, you might compliment a manager's choice in hiring a particular employee because of that employee's wonderful performance. By doing so and by couching your communication in such a way that the manager knows that you are complimenting his judgment in the hiring process, he will then have his self-esteem boosted.

7. Concentrate on the person in whom you are trying to build self-esteem. For instance, if this individual is one of your best friends, turn most of the conversation to him, his accomplishments, his interests, and the events of his week. Do not spend a great deal of time talking about another best friend, how wonderful that individual is, and how much she has achieved that week. Sometimes, quite innocently, we deflate the ego of the other person when we enhance the value of a third party. Also, this technique of

high praise is used by manipulative individuals in order to "put down" the person at hand and to build the self-esteem of the one who is giving the praise. Be careful that you do not intentionally do that to someone else. If someone does that to you, be aware that one of two motives could exist—unintentional praise of the third party or intentional, manipulative behavior.

Effective power phrases to build self-esteem in other people are:

- "Congratulations!"
- "Great!"
- "Good job!"
- "I'm proud of you!"
- "I love you!"

TRUST

Relationships built on jealousy and restriction fail. When two people allow each other freedom, the relationship can grow and prosper. This is true of business associates, friends, and married couples.

No one person can ever satisfy all your relationship needs, and you cannot satisfy all needs of another person. Healthy relationships are built when friendships are diversified. Marriages are often suffocated when one mate expects the other to be all things and to satisfy all physical and emotional needs. The marriage will be more successful if there are multiple relationships and bondings for both mates outside the marriage.

Marie G. confided in me that her husband does not provide the nurturing intimacy that she needs. Recently, when she had a conflict at work, she did not care that her husband solved the problem. She just wanted him to hold her, listen, nurture, pet her, and tell her that everything would be all right (whether or not he actually felt it would). Instead, her husband told her that she was silly to worry about such petty squabbles at work. He suggested that she just forget about it and watch a little television. She interpreted his behavior as non-nurturing and insensitive. However, rather than be upset with her husband, Marie understands that he simply does not have the ability to provide the sensitivity that she needs. To satisfy that need she confides in her best friend who has a relater profile. Her friend will listen for hours, cry with her and gently hug her, and as she does, comfort her by telling her everything will be "O.K." With this outlet, Marie has a happier marriage and no longer expects behavior of her husband that he is uncomfortable in providing.

Another trust involved in relationship building comes from having faith in your feelings with no expectations from the other person. If you like someone enough to invest in a relationship with them, do not expect those feelings and rewards to be returned. Just as good returns are reaped from most investments, good feelings will normally be returned to you. However, the idea is to not expect them but to bask in the joy when a favorable relationship is formed. When you can trust yourself enough to give away your feelings without destroying your ego if no return comes your way, you are an emotionally healthy person. By giving yourself unconditionally to relationships without threat to your self-esteem, you will, in the end, reap untold happiness and reward.

Power phrases that will be helpful in strengthening relationship trust are:

- "I'll do the chores tonight. Why don't you go out with a group of friends?"
- "I'm here whenever you need me."
- "Here is a surprise although I realize there is no special occasion."

In Conclusion . . .

In the New Age, money alone cannot provide the peace of mind which we all seek. Though material things are important, spiritual needs are met through bondings with others. By investing in relationships, you will increase the value of your life and will reap unexpected rewards unknown in previous generations.

Summary:

1. The materialistic economy of the Second Wave caused much psychological and emotional deprivation.
2. True peace of mind is accomplished only when there is a solid balance between the material and spiritual well-being in an individual's life.
3. No matter what role you play in your career or your personal life, the ability to develop and maintain solid relationships will be a determinant of your success in the New Age.
4. To reap a true unexpected return from relationships, it is important to I-N-V-E-S-T. This acronym stands for:
    - respect for **individualism**
    - meeting of **needs**
    - **values** synchronization

- establishment of **empathy**
- building of **self-esteem**
- **trust**

5. Relationship development begins with attitude when you release your "self" to relate. It is enhanced through communication resulting in mutual understanding and is solidified through specific actions.

Chapter 11

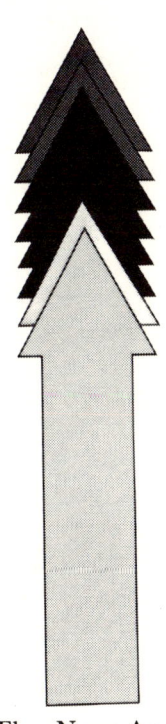

The Beginning

We should all be concerned about the future because we will all have to spend the rest of our lives there.
— Charles F. Kettering

The New Age is being born! Never has there been more opportunity for prosperity in America. The exciting part of this whole scenario is that you hold the freedom to prosper through your own power and ingenuity.

Because the economy is operating under a new set of evolving rules, you have the choice of being a rule maker or a rule follower. Prosperity in the New Age requires more than being in the right place at the right time. It requires positioning yourself in the right place *before* the right time.

By anticipating the effects of the seven economic conditions on your life, career, and family, you will be better prepared to take advantage of opportunities in the New Age.

You have a definite role in the success of America's new economy. During the next fifteen years, many decisions will be made about America's future in the twenty-first century. Our country's very survival will depend on its ability to move forward and to mature into the New Age Economy. Many leaders are calling for America to go back to the productivity and quality of work of previous generations. However, we cannot go *back*. We must move *forward* to new opportunities and must allow new developing countries to perform many Second Wave tasks. History does not repeat itself; instead, our country is life cycling from beginning to infinity. Looking back is healthy only to glean lessons of experience. At the same time, it can be dangerous to extrapolate from the past because those rules for success and prosperity may be counterproductive. By learning from the present, we can better deal with the future. By applying power positioning strategies, we can assure more peace of mind — personally, financially, and spiritually. Research indicates that peace of mind is pursued as the first priority of success in the New Age.

During the immediate future, the challenges are great and the rewards can be bountiful.

As you begin your future, please share with me a personal philosophy for New Age prosperity. These principles will work — if you will.

LOOK AHEAD.
Vision assures hope for tomorrow.

LAUGH.
Merriment produces sunshine for the soul.

LOVE.
Caring is a gift for all seasons.

LEARN.
Knowledge fuels the fires of growth and freedom.

LABOR.
Work exchanges for self-respect and human dignity.

LIFT UP.
A positive spirit buffers the storms of life.

LET GO.
Freedom from fear is the passport to peace.[1]

Notes

Quotes at the beginning of each chapter are taken from the Bible, King James Version, World Publishing, and from *The Treasure Chest*, Charles L. Wallis, ed., Harper & Row, 1965.

Chapter One: The Future is Rushing into the Present

1. Though the situation is real, the flight number of the jetliner is fictitious.
2. Quote is from *Megatrends* by John Naisbitt, Warner Books, 1982.

Chapter Two: The Past is Separating from the Present

1. References are to *The Third Wave* by Alvin Toffler, Bantam Books, 1981. Other than First and Second Wave terminology and some dates for waves, ideas on all three economies are those of the author.
2. Information on Federal Reserve System from the *Federal Reserve System, Purposes and Functions* by Board of Governors of the Federal Reserve System, Washington, D.C., 1984.
3. Information on Kondratieff Wave concluded from: Joseph P. Martino, "Does the Kondratieff Wave Really Exist?" *The Futurist*, February 1985.
4. Craig S. Vollard, "Kondratieff's Long-Wave Cycle," *The Futurist*, February 1985.
5. Paul P. Craig and Kenneth E. F. Watt, "The Kondratieff Cycle and War: How Close is the Connection," *The Futurist*, April 1985.
6. Paul Hawken, *The Next Economy*, Ballantine Books, New York, 1983.

7. Statistics from *U. S. Chamber of Commerce, Employee Benefits Historical Data*, U. S. Chamber Research Center, Washington, D.C., 1981.
8. *Money* magazine, "Americans and Their Money," Time, Inc., 1984.
9. Producing a generation: Daniel Yankelovich, *New Rules*, Bantam Books, Inc., 1982.

Chapter Three: The New Age Economy

1. Good explanation of interaction of people, energy, and capital in *The Next Economy* (listed earlier).
2. Far East information from Scott W. Erickson, "The Transition Between Eras," *The Futurist*, August 1985.
3. Information on acceleration of change is from IBM GUIDE meeting, 1976.
4. "Surveys . . . " John Diebold, "New Challenges for the Information Age," *The Futurist*, June 1985.
5. Census data on older Americans based on American Association of Retired Persons, "A Profile of Older Americans," 1984.
6. Philosophy of Dr. Jonas Salk from "A Conversation with Jonas Salk," *Psychology Today*, March 1983.
7. Eighteen minutes statement heard in sermon of Billy Graham, September 1985, Anaheim, California.
8. Baby boomers as 54% of the work force by 1990. "Here Comes the Baby-Boomers," *U. S. News and World Report*, November 5, 1984.
9. General ideas on baby boom population growth from "What the Baby Boomers Will Buy Next," by Geoffrey Calvin, *Fortune*, October 15, 1984.
10. Materials important to the Pentagon from Kiplinger Washington Editors, *The Kiplinger Washington Letter*, September 9, 1985.
11. Information on coal gasification from Bruce Nichols, "Shell Testing Process," *Dallas Morning News*, August 28, 1985.

Chapter Four: Seven New Age Economic Conditions

1. Wage data from Charles McMillion, "Automate, Emigrate, or Evaporate," *The Futurist*, April 1983.
2. Household products statistics from *The Washington Post*, "Giant Step Downward," printed in *Dallas Times Herald*, August 7, 1985.
3. Summary on retailing from Donna Steph Hansard, "Ward to End Catalog Business," *Dallas Morning News*, August 3, 1985, and "It's a Jungle Out There, Zale Exec Warns Retailers," *Dallas Morning News*, April 28, 1985. Also from "Dallas Retailing," a *Dallas, Inc.* article by Sally Bell, *Dallas Times Herald*, September 2, 1985.
4. Global automobile sales discussed by Robert B. Reich, *The Next American Frontier*, Penguin Books, 1984.
5. Interview with Roger Smith in *Deloitte, Haskins, and Sells Review*, April 1, 1985.

6. International furniture market from "International Furniture Fair Planned for Dallas," Ruth Eyre, *Dallas Times Herald*, July 9, 1985.

7. Competition in options trading, Janet Novack, "Competing for Sales," *Dallas Times Herald*, June 8, 1985.

8. Airlines competition from "Airlines Warfare," Robert Reed, *Dallas, Inc.*, *Dallas Times Herald*, June 24, 1985.

9. Broadcasting industry information from Alvin P. Sanoff, "TV Tries to Sharpen Focus on its Viewers," *U. S. News and World Report*, September 23, 1985.

10. Public television, "Ch. 13 Steps Toward Commercialism," David Zurawik, *Dallas Times Herald*, August 14, 1985.

11. Banking summary in Charles P. Alexander, "Banking Takes A Beating," *Time*, December 3, 1984.

12. Bank failure statistics from D. W. Nauss, "Bank Failures May Grow," *Dallas Times Herald*, February 6, 1985.

13. *The American Banker* poll in "Banking Takes A Beating" (listed earlier).

14. Views on interstate banking from Paul Volcker in "Fed Backs Interstate Banking," *Dallas Times Herald*, April 25, 1985.

15. Foreign banks in the U. S., Alfred King, "Japanese Bank Plans Dallas Office," *Dallas Times Herald*, August 13, 1985. Also "Banking on More Than Charm," Polly Ross Hughes, *Dallas Morning News*, September 16, 1985.

16. Information on the textile industry by Donna Steph Hansard, "U. S. Manufacturers, Retailers at Odds Over Clothing Imports," *Dallas Morning News*, September 17, 1985.

17. Competition in the steel industry, Kathryn Jones, "LTV To Shut Steel Works, Lay Off 1,300," *Dallas Times Herald*, May 18, 1985, and *The Next American Frontier* (listed earlier).

18. Communications information from "Stiffer Competition Taking Toll on AT&T" by Jim Mitchell, *Dallas Morning News*, August 24, 1985.

19. Discussion on special offers by hospitals from "Cut-rate: Hospitals' Competition for Patients Translates into Big Savings for Many," *Dallas Morning News*, June 17, 1985, and "Hospitals Compete for Affluent Patients By Offering Luxury Suites and Hot Tubs," *The Wall Street Journal*, February 3, 1986.

20. Information on competition among different types of health insurance and the power of the hospital chains from "Medical Turmoil: Four Large Hospital Chains React to Prospect of Declining Profits with Innovations," *The Wall Street Journal*, Summer 1985.

21. Doctors' and dentists' crunch of competition as discussed in "Health Care Losing Glow of Prosperity" by Scott Burns, *Dallas Morning News*, August 11, 1985.

22. " . . . industries excelling in productivity and growth" from Kiplinger Washington Editors, *The Kiplinger Washington Letter*, August 16, 1985.

23. Information on Dual Drilling, Joe Simnacher, "Dual Drilling Finds Fertile Ground, Gulf in Depressed Times," *Dallas Morning News*, August 14, 1985.

24. American farmland data from wire reports in *Dallas Times Herald*, June 8, 1985.

25. The ripple effect, Robert Guenther, "More Homeowners in Financial Trouble Opt for Foreclosure," *The Wall Street Journal*, February 1, 1985.

26. Short shelf-life from *National Report for Training and Development*, American Society for Training and Development, Vol. 11, No. 21, December 5, 1984.

27. Blue-collar jobs from Ben Bova and Robert Weil, eds., "The Business Sector," *Omni Future Almanac*, World Almanac Publications, New York, 1983.

28. Early retirement programs cited in "Early Retirement Two-edged Sword for Employees," Jonathan Peterson, *Los Angeles Times Syndicate*, June 1985.

29. Merger statistics from "The Personal Impact When Firms Are Taken Over," Ron Scherer and Linda K. Lanier, *U. S. News and World Report*, December 3, 1984.

30. Job security: "Apple Layoffs Overdue, Analysts Say," June 15, 1985, and "Split Not Likely To Spoil Apple," September 22, 1985, *Dallas Morning News*.

31. "Approximately 20,000 total workers . . .," Jim Mitchell, "Tough Times Break Through High-tech's Imaginary Shield," *Dallas Morning News*, June 22, 1985.

32. "In the energy industry alone . . .," Ron Scherer and Linda K. Lanier (listed earlier).

33. Information on midlevel management, *Business Week*, Special Report, April 25, 1983.

34. Outmoded jobs cited in *Omni Future Almanac* (listed earlier).

35. McDonnell Douglas from *The Kiplinger Washington Letter*, October 4, 1985.

36. "To speed table service . . ." *The Kiplinger Washington Letter*, May 31, 1985.

37. Diagnosis machine from *The Kiplinger Washington Letter*, Kiplinger Washington Editors, 1985.

38. Voice computer programming in "Computers' Next Frontiers," Manuel Schiffres, *U. S. News and World Report*, August 26, 1985.

39. Food, health, and beauty product development, *SME Digest*, Vol. 1, June 1985, Sales and Marketing Executives International.

40. Computer profits in "Computers' Next Frontiers" (listed earlier).

41. Employees look out for themselves taken from Thomas F. Oboyle's "Loyalty Ebbs at Many Companies as Employees Grow Disillusioned," *The Wall Street Journal*, July 11, 1985.

42. Discussion on corporate pensions from "As Corporate 'Raids' On Pensions Pick Up Steam," Carey W. English, *U. S. News and World Report*, July 29, 1985, and "More Firms Allowing Employees To Defer Bonuses To Save Taxes," Karen Slater, *The Wall Street Journal*, September 16, 1985.

43. Divorce statistics from Stanford University in Robert Runde, "Cutting Up A Family's Finances," *Money*, November 1983.

44. Information on debtor nation, Martin Crutsinger, "U. S. Marks 1985 By Plunging Into Debtor-Nation Category," *Associated Press*, March 1985.

45. "Five times the assets . . ." *The Next Economy* (listed earlier).

Chapter Five: Power Positioning

1. Data on General Motors' purchase of Hughes Aircraft and EDS from "Perot and Smith: Capitalism's Odd Couple, *Dallas Times Herald*, July 14, 1985.

2. Glass Savers, Inc. information from"Firm Repairs Windshield 'Pings,' " *Dallas/Fort Worth Business Journal*, April 29, 1985.

3. Discussion on Wang Laboratories from "Wang Visits Dallas Partner," *Dallas Times Herald*, October 2, 1985.

4. Reference to long-range research and development at Sun Exploration cited in "Sun Technology Center Planned," *Dallas/Fort Worth Business Journal*, April 29, 1985.

5. Joint ventures of GTE Telenet/Intec/Sumitomo Corporation cited in September 28, 1985 issue of *Dallas Times Herald*. Partnerships of ABC/Hearst, AT&T/N. V. Phillips, IBM/CBS/Sears found in "Friendly Ties: More Companies Make Alliances To Expand Into Related Businesses" by John Marcom, Jr., *The Wall Street Journal*, November 8, 1985. "NBC, Texas Affiliates Test News Sharing," Bob Brock, *Dallas Times Herald*, March 23, 1985.

6. New emphasis on human capital: GM cited earlier in "Perot and Smith," July 14, 1985; Coca-Cola from Cotten Timberlake's Associated Press article, "Consumers' Negative Reaction Forced Coke Change," *Dallas Times Herald*, July 14, 1985.

7. Results of Federal Reserve Bank of Atlanta from "Winning Companies Emphasize Innovation, Creativity, Study Finds," from *Orlando Sentinel* reprinted in *Dallas Times Herald*, May 9, 1985.

Chapter Six: Declare Your Independence

1. Information on Elmer Doolin (Fritos), Jimmy Dewar (Twinkies), and Fred Waring (Waring Blender) from *Top Sellers, U.S.A.: Success Stories Behind America's Best-Selling Products From Alka-Seltzer To Zippo* by Molly McGrath, William Morrow, 1983.

2. Creation of Tofu, Time, Inc. and David Mintz taken from *"Small Businesses: Beating the Odds,"* by Mark J. Estren in *Dial*, August 1984.

3. Marketing tests data on soft drinks, juices, etc. found in *Los Angeles Times* article, "Designers Go For A Package Deal," by Kathleen Day, reprinted in the *Dallas Times Herald* on March 19, 1985.

4. Sense of humor performance information from "Humor on the Job," *Dallas Morning News*, February 25, 1986. Their source was *Working Woman*.

Chapter Seven: Anticipate Tomorrow's Business World

1. Information on "The Fabulous Future, America in 1980" from Trust and Investment Update, Republic National Bank Trust Department, January 1980 (copyright 1980 by M. A. Co.)

2. "Future Immigration Key To U. S. Growth," *Dallas Inc.*, *Dallas Times Herald*, Peter Francese, January 13, 1986.

3. Japanese investments in the U. S. from International Writers Service and UPI by Nobuko Hara published in the *Dallas Times Herald*, November 17, 1985, and from "New Frontiers: Japanese Real Estate Purchases Portend Land Rush, Analysts Say," Steve Brown, *Dallas Morning News*, October 28, 1985.

4. Productivity survey results from Robert Half's" 'Time Theft,' America's Biggest Crime," *The Financial Planner*, May 1982.

5. Data on health care benefits from "Alternative Health Plans Reduce Employers' Costs" by Jube Shiver, Jr., *Los Angeles Times* reprinted in the *Dallas Times Herald*, October 27, 1985.

6. Diversification in the tobacco industry and law firms from "Tobacco Companies Diversity," *The Washington Post* reprinted in the *Dallas Times Herald*, October 25, 1985, and from *The Wall Street Journal*, "Law Firms Aren't Simply for Law as Attempts to Diversify Begin," November 18, 1985.

7. Predictions on video discs and electronic workstations from *Omni Future Almanac* cited in Chapter 4 notes. SRI International data from *Brave New Workplace* by Robert Howard, Viking Press, 1985.

8. Threshold Messaging System information from the Associated Press reprinted in "Careful Whispers: Stores, Offices Use Subtle Warnings to Broadcast Honesty," *Dallas Times Herald*, May 27, 1985.

9. "Robot Police: Georgia Firm Offers Novel Security Device" by Steve Klinerman, *Dallas Times Herald*, October 2, 1985.

10. Information on manufacturing robots in "Redefining the Workplace: Employees Work From Home and Robots Romp in Factories," Kathryn Jones, *Dallas Times Herald*, October 27, 1985.

11. Employees working at home from Telecommuters Make Better Employees as cited in "Runzheimer On Cars and Living Costs," June 1985, Vol. 19, No. 2, Runzheimer International, Rochester, Wisconsin.

12. Complications in the automated workplace are discussed in "The Unfinished Revolution," *A Special Report: Technology in the Workplace*, *The Wall Street Journal*, September 16, 1985.

13. Trade and service industry statistics from "The U. S. Since World War II," *U. S. News and World Report*, August 5, 1985.
14. Survey data from Stanard and Associates discussed in "Workers Becoming Less Satisfied With Jobs," Sally Bell, *Dallas Times Herald*, December 25, 1985.
15. Information on "has beens" from "Finished at Forty," *The Wall Street Journal, Technology Careers*, September 16, 1985.
16. Workers with substantive skills identified as elite workers by J. Walter Thompson ad agency in "The New-Collar Class," *U. S. News and World Report*, September 16, 1985.
17. Status on U. S. population with college education obtained from Jean Coupe based on a U. S. national news report, 1985.
18. Dean Raymond E. Miles's proposed new system of business education from *The California Management Review*, Spring 1985, and summarized in "Educator Recommends New Course for Business Schools," *Dallas Morning News*, July 5, 1985.
19. Information on graying employees from "Snapshot of a Changing America," *Time*, September 2, 1985, and from *A Practitioner's Guide for Training Older Workers* by Brenda Lester, National Commission for Employment Policy, Washington, D. C., 1984.
20. Older workers at Texas Refinery Corporation and Travelers Insurance Company cited in "Age Proving Itself as Workplace Asset," *Dallas Morning News*, December 8, 1985. Data also from Miriam Rozen's article, "Managers Will Face Legal Issues in '86," *Dallas, Inc., Dallas Times Herald*, January 6, 1985.
21. Second Wave industry executives face loss of employment cited in "Older Execs Fighting Odds in Job Market," *Dallas Morning News*, December 8, 1985.
22. Information on more trust between employees and company found in *The New Achievers*, Perry Pascarella, the Free Press (A Division of Macmillan, Inc.), 1984.
23. Statistics indicating flexibility in the work place cited in Ray Alvareztorres's Business Watch column, "Work Schedules Turn Flexible," *Dallas, Inc., Dallas Times Herald*, September 23, 1985. Information also taken from "More Employees Giving Part-Time Hours A Workout," *The Christian Science Monitor* by Marilyn Gardner, September 1985, and "Older Workers Find They're Still Needed in the Corporate World" by Bill Crawford, *AARP News Bulletin*, February 1986.
24. Employee sabbaticals concept from "Sabbaticals Spread From Campus To Business," *U. S. News and World Report*, January 28, 1985.
25. Data on employees' raises based on productivity from *The Wall Street Journal*, "Many Companies Now Base Workers' Raises On Their Productivity," Carrie Dolan, November 15, 1985.
26. Information from Miriam Rozen, "Managers Will Face Legal Issues in '86," *Dallas, Inc., Dallas Times Herald*, January 6, 1986, and

from "Can Companies Kill?" by Berkeley Rice in *Psychology Today*, June 1981.

27. The changing nature of work from the *Omni Future Almanac* (cited earlier in Chapter 7 notes).

28. Bureau of Labor Statistics on new jobs from "The Shifting Workforce," *The Dallas Morning News*, November 14, 1985.

29. Data on job displacement from "Technology and the Changing World of Work" by Fred Best in *The Futurist*, April 1984, and from "Robots and Job Loss," *The Futurist*, April 1985.

30. Career listings from:

- "Redefining the Workplace: Employees Work From Home and Robots Romp in Factories," Kathryn Jones, *Dallas Times Herald*, October 27, 1985.
- "Snapshot of a Changing America," *Time*, September 2, 1985.
- *Omni Future Almanac* (cited earlier in Chapter 7 notes).
- "Jobs for the Future," *U. S. News and World Report*, December 23, 1985.

Chapter Eight: Develop Resource Connectors

1. References to Andrew Carnegie and others from *Think and Grow Rich* by Napoleon Hill, original copyright 1937, republished by Wilshire Book Company, 1978.

2. Career connector networking from "Networking Said Key to Success" by Melinda Zemper, *Morning Press*, Carlsbad, California, October 16, 1983.

3. Ideas under intimacy connectors from:

- Erich Fromm, *The Art of Loving*, Harper & Brothers, 1956.
- "Poll Finds Women Want Tenderness More Than Sex" and Ann Landers's "Responses to Sex Poll Surprise Annie," *Dallas Morning News*, January 15, 1985.
- Karl A. Menninger, *Love Against Hate*, Harcourt Brace Jovanovich, 1959.

4. Information for spiritual connectors from *Becoming: Basic Considerations for a Psychology of Personality* by Gordon W. Allport, Yale University Press, 1955, and "Tribute: Airman's Sonnet" from *New York Times*, January 30, 1986.

Chapter Nine: Prepare for Predictable Uncertainty

1. Difficulty in predicting economy from "The Economist's New Clothes" by Douglas L. Bendt and Carolyne Lochhead in *Fortune*, April 1, 1985.

2. Uncertainty predicted in the 1980s from *Changing Times*, "The Rest of the 80's," January 1984, and from "How to Make Yourself Financially Secure," a special report from *Money*, October 1983, by Marlys Harris.

3. Statistics on financial planners in the U. S. from "Watch Your Assets," Janet Bamford and William G. Flanagan, *Forbes*, October 8, 1984.

4. Data on New Age corporate world from "A New Era For Management," *Business Week*, April 25, 1983.

5. Disability insurance information taken from "Loopholes, Pitfalls & Gobbledygook in Disability Insurance" by Martin Steinhausen in August 7, 1977, *Chicago Tribune* and in "Disability Insurance a Must . . ." by Patricia Estes in *Sylvia Porter's Personal Finance*, June 1984.

6. Discussion of disability and Social Security from *Make Your Money Grow*, Theodore J. Miller, ed., Kiplinger Washington Editors, Inc., 1984. Later discussion of H.M.O.s and P.P.O.s, same source.

7. Information on three points of coverage taken from "Disability Insurance: Will You Be Wiped Out If You're Laid Up?" in *Medical Economics*, November 7, 1977.

8. Traditional health insurance plan data from *The Handbook of Personal Insurance*, Research Institute of America, 1983.

9. Power of attorney discussion from "When You Need to Use an Attorney," *Changing Times*, November 1980.

10. Information on living trust from "Watch Your Assets" (listed earlier in this chapter's notes).

11. *Inter vivos* trust discussion taken from Stephan R. Leimberg, et.al., "Trusts — Inter vivos," *The Tools and Techniques of Estate Planning*, 4th ed., National Underwriter Company, Cincinnati, Ohio, 1982.

12. Homeowners insurance information taken from *Home Insurance Basics*, Insurance Information Institute, 1981, and *How to Protect What's Yours* by Nancy Golonka, Acropolis Books Ltd., 1983.

13. Basic auto insurance coverage from *Auto Insurance Basics*, Insurance Information Institute, 1980.

14. Other auto insurance hints from *Planning for a One-Way Trip: Pre-retirement Planning Strategies That Keep On Working After You Have Quit*, Carolyn Pitts Corbin, Carolyn Corbin, Inc., 1981.

15. Umbrella liability insurance discussion from "What If You're Sued for a Million?" in *Changing Times*, December 1984.

16. Information on comprehensive personal liability insurance taken from David L. Bickelhaupt's *General Insurance*, Richard D. Irwin, Inc., Homewood, Illinois, 1979.

17. Discussion on impending marriage routine business taken from "Financial Planning: A Lifetime Affair," Arthur H. Rogoff, *Sylvia Porter's Personal Finance*, April 1984.

18. Prenuptial agreement information from Margaret Mahar, "Striking a Deal Before Tying the Knot," *Money*, January 1984, and Neal A. Kuyer, "The Business of Remarriage," *Dynamic Years*, September – October 1984.

19. Material to gather before prenuptial agreement discussed in

"Late Marriage and the Law" by Janet Lowe, *Modern Maturity*, August–September 1980.

20. Female-headed household statistics from *Time*, September 2, 1985 (cited in Chapter 7 notes).

21. Statistic on teenage expenses from "Financial Planning: A Lifetime Affair" mentioned in earlier notes of this chapter.

22. "Aside from a house . . . " quote and statistics taken from *How To Put Your Child Through College Without Going Broke*, Inese Rudzitis, ed., The Research Institute of America, Inc., New York, 1985.

23. Information on divorce from *Money*, November 1983 (listed in Chapter 4 notes).

24. Chart 5 and Chart 6 adapted from *Five Steps To Financial Success*, Carolyn Pitts Corbin, Carolyn Corbin, Inc., Dallas, Texas, 1984.

25. Aging parent information taken from *Sylvia Porter's Personal Finance*, April 1984 (listed earlier in this chapter's notes).

26. Statistics on people over sixty-five from the White House Conference on Aging, Washington, D.C., 1981, published in *Park Cities Baptist Church Journal*, February 1, 1985.

27. Baby boomers' view of parents from the American Council of Life AMERICAN DEMOGRAPHICS (5/84) in *Psychology Today*, April 1985.

28. Information on wills taken from "Do I Need a Will?" published by the State Bar of Texas, Austin, Texas, 1981.

29. Information on Natural Death Act and donation of body parts from *Planning Your Estate with Wills, Probate, and Taxes*, Dennis Clifford and Jim Simmons, Attorneys at Law, Nolo Press Book, Addison-Wesley Publishing Company, 1981.

30. Ideas for New Age financial strategies from "Retirement Planning Table," Sam Beller, CLU and Sam Sugar, CLU on behalf of Diversified Programs, Inc. found in *Financial and Estate Planning*, Commerce Clearing House, 1981.

Chapter Ten: Release Yourself to Relate

1. Statistics from Carnegie Institute of Technology taken from *The Friendship Factor* by Alan Loy McGinnis, Augsburg Publishing House, Minneapolis, 1979.

2. Leadership traits from *Conduct Expected*, Bill Lareau, New Century Publishers, Piscataway, New Jersey, 1985, and from *Personal Report for the Executive*, Research Institute of America, New York, September 17, 1985.

3. New Age sales information taken from Theodore Levitt's "After the Sale is Over . . .," *Harvard Business Review*, September–October, 1983.

4. Material from Paul L. Wachtel, *The Poverty of Affluence: A Psychological Portrait of the American Way of Life*, The Free Press, New York, 1983, taken from a book review in *The Journal of Consumer Affairs*, Timothy E. Moore, Summer 1985.

5. Information on personal styles and for the I-N-V-E-S-T acronym from Carolyn Pitts Corbin, *New Age Leadership*, Carolyn Corbin, Inc., Dallas, Texas, 1985.

6. Monkey contact comfort research by Harry F. Harlow, "The Nature of Love," *The American Psychologist*, Volume 13, 1958.

7. Research on handling and petting of rats by Otto Weininger, W. J. McClellan, and R. K. Arima, "Gentling and Weight Gain in Albino Rats," *Canadian Journal of Psychology*, Volume 8, 1954.

8. Infant mortality in orphanages research by M. F. Ashley Montagu, *The Direction of Human Development*, Harper & Brothers, New York, 1955.

9. Information on participatory management taken from "Middle Managers and Supervisors Resist Moves to More Participatory Management," Leonard M. Apcar, *The Wall Street Journal*, September 16, 1985.

10. Notes on adult attention span, retention, and involvement from Northwestern Mutual Life Career School, Milwaukee, Wisconsin, 1979.

Chapter Eleven: The Beginning

1. Closing remarks from "Seven L's for Living" by Carolyn Pitts Corbin, copyright 1985.

Index

A

ABC (American Broadcasting Company), 42, 63
Advance Security, 100
age discrimination, 109, 110
agents, in self-promotion, 86, 89
aging parents, 129, 155–157
agricultural economy, 7–9, 20, 47
airline industry, 41
Allport, Gordon W., 122
American Airlines, 50
American Association of Retired Persons (AARP), 27, 156
American Banker, The, 43
American International Furniture Fair, 41
American Telephone and Telegraph (AT&T), 44, 45, 63
American Textile Manufacturers Institute, 43
"Americans and Their Money," 14
appearance, 77–78
Apple Computer, 50
Arima, R. K., 175
Arnold and Porter, 98
articulation skills, 83
artificial intelligence, 46
Atlantic Richfield, 50
attention span of average adult, 181
attorney, 128, 129, 147, 158, 160, 161
automobile industry, 40–41
automobile insurance, 143–145

B

baby boom generation, 13, 26, 27, 28, 33, 52, 53, 104, 155
Bangladesh wages, 39
Bank Holding Company Act amendments of 1970, 11
Bank of America Corporation, 50, 109
banker, 129, 154
Banking Act of 1935, 11
banking industry, 42–43, 48
Bell, Sally, 40
Best's Insurance Reports, 128, 137, 144, 159
Boe, Ann, 114
Borman, Frank, 41
broad interest span, 82–83
broadcasting industry, 42
broker, 129, 155
budget deficit, 55
Burbank, Luther, 113
Burroughs, John, 113
business world of tomorrow, 95–112

C

California Management Review, The, 104
Canadian Conference of Catholic Bishops, 165
career connectors, 114–115
career counselors, 73
career interruption, 131–132
Career Networks, 114
career obsolescence, 51
careers of promise, 111

careers to avoid, 111
Carnegie, Andrew, 113
Carnegie Institute of Technology, 164
CBS (Columbia Broadcasting System), 42, 63
certified public accountant (CPA), 128, 161
chartered life underwriter (CLU), 128
Chicago Board Options Exchange, 41
children, 129, 148–150
Churchill, Winston, 76
Coca-Cola, 64
cognitive workers, 101
College for Financial Planning, Denver, 128
college planning and costs, 149–150
communication: barriers, 179; feeling level of, 183; intellectual level of, 183; involvement, 178–183; levels, 183; nonverbal, 77–78; surface level of, 183
communications industry, 44–45
community work, 89
competition, 23, 33, 149
competition, global and domestic, 38–46, 131
competitor profile, 168–170
Complete Guide to Long Term Care, A, 156
comprehensive personal liability, 146
computer industry, 44, 45, 46, 47, 50, 52, 62, 100
consolidated part-time, 107
consultants, use of, 98, 108
consumptive lifestyle, 10, 14, 28
Continental Bakeries, 75
conversational skills, 81–82
Corning Glassworks, 177
corporate strategies, 61–66
corporation (a major economic unit of Second Wave), 10
curriculum development, 103, 104

D

Data Resources, Inc., 44
death, 157–161
death certificate, 160
debtor nation, 54
deferred compensation plans (401-k), 155
Deloitte, Haskins, and Sells, 40
demographic explosion, 13–14
demographic structure, shifting, 26–29, 33
Depository Institutions Deregulation and Monetary Control Act of 1980, 11
Desiderata, The, 118
Dewar, Jimmy, 75
Diebold, John, 25
disability, 129, 132–138
disability insurance, 134–138
divorce, 53, 150–151
Doolin, Elmer, 75
Downwardly Mobile Professionals (DMPs), 102
dual-career families, 32
Dual Drilling Company, 47
DuPont, 50

E

Eastern Airlines, 41
economic cycles, predictable, 11–12, 124
economic factors cause economic conditions, 20–22
economic supremacy, 24
economy, convulsive, 54–55, 124, 125
economy, importance of, 5
Edison, Thomas, 113
educated labor, 103–104
Eggers Industries, 178
Eisenhower, Dwight D., 80–81
Electronic Data Systems (EDS), 62, 63

Index 205

electronic work stations, 99
empathy, 178–183
employee benefits, 13, 102, 106, 108
Employee Benefits Historical Data (U.S. Chamber of Commerce), 13
employee-driven, 105–110
employee rights, 109
employee satisfaction, 102
Employee Stock Ownership Plans (ESOPs), 155
employees, graying, 104–105
energy crisis, 27
energy source alternatives, 34, 48
"enhanced underwriting messages," 42
entertainer profile, 170–171
exchange, means of, 35

F

Fabulous Future, America in 1980, The, 96
family (a major economic unit of First Wave), 8
Federal Depositors Insurance Corporation (FDIC), 48
Federal Reserve Act of 1913, 10
Federal Reserve Bank of Atlanta, 64
Federal Reserve System, 10–11
fiber optics, 46
financial planner, 127, 128, 158, 159
financial professionals team, 127–129
financial services, diversified, 55
financial strategies, New Age, 129–131, 133, 161–163
Firestone, Harvey, 113
Firestone Tire & Rubber, 50
First Wave Economy, 7–9, 21
flextime, 107
Forbes 100 list, 49
Ford, Henry, 113
foreign industry, 97
Forrester, Jay, 11, 12
Fortune, 96
Frito-Lay, 75
Fritos, 75

Fromm, Erich, 118
Full Employment and Balanced Growth Act of 1978, 11
furniture industry, 41
"Future of Business Education, The," 103
Futurist, 25

G

General Foods, 61, 98
General Motors, 40, 41, 49, 56, 62, 63, 64, 109
Generalized Skills Professionals (GSPs), 103
geographic areas, variation in, 47
Georgia State University, 113
Getty Oil/Texaco, 61
Glass Savers, Inc., 62
goal-directed energy, 80
Goodyear Tire and Rubber Company, 98
government (a major economic unit of Second Wave), 10, 13
GTE Telenet, 62
Gulf/Chevron Corporations, 61

H

Harlow, Harry, 175
Harvard Business Review, 165
health care industry, 45
health insurance, 45, 138–140, 151
health maintenance organization (HMO), 45, 138, 139
Hewlett Packard Company, 109
"High Flight," 123
Hill, Napoleon, 113
homeowners insurance, 142, 143
Honeywell, Inc., 109
household products industry, 39
housing foreclosures, 48
Hughes Aircraft, 62
human capital, 56
humor, 82
Hurst Corporation, 63

I

IBM (International Business Machines), 32, 44, 63
immigration, 97
import-export deficit, 54
indipreneurship, 69, 70
individual responsibility, 52–53, 68, 114, 161
individual retirement accounts (IRAs), 53, 154–155, 157, 159
individual strategies, 65
individualism, 166–173
industrial age, 9–10
industrial emphasis, 30–33
industry units, variation among, 46
industry units, variation within, 46
infant death rate, 175
information-driven society, 31, 32
information economy, 49
institutional dependency, 13
institutional dominance, 29–30, 33–34
insurance agent, 128, 143, 146, 147, 158, 159, 160
insurance, auto, 143–145
insurance, homeowners, 142, 143
Intec, 63
InteCom, 62
inter vivos trust, 141, 160
interdependence of Second Wave, 31–32
International Association of Drilling Contractors, 47
International Association of Financial Planners, 128
International Banking Act of 1978, 11
international debt structure, 55
International Training and Communication, 83
intimacy connectors, 118
I-N-V-E-S-T, 166
investing for retirement goals, 153–155

investments: and savings program, 70–71, 129, 130, 132; conservative, 162; diversified, 161–162; higher risk, 162; safe, 162

J

J. Walter Thompson ad agency, 103
Japanese investments in the U.S., 97
job obsolescence, 49
job relocation, 131
job security, 49, 50–51
job sharing, 106

K

Kennedy, John F., 26
K-Mart, 42
Kondratieff, Nikolai D., 11, 12
Kondratieff Wave, 11, 12, 65

L

labor unions, 9
Landers, Ann, 118
landowners, 8
Lareau, Bill, 165
Laterally Mobile Professionals (LMPs), 102, 104
leadership skills, 80, 90, 165
letters of commendation, 86–87
Levitt, Theodore, 165
liability lawsuit, 109, 110, 143, 145–146
Lincoln, Abraham, 122
listener involvement, 181–182
listening: barriers, 179; improvement, 179–180; through your eyes, 180
living trust, 140–141
Lombardi, Vince, 74
loss to home/other structures, 141–143
Love Against Hate, 118

M

Magee, John Gillespie, 123
management, participatory, 177–178
marriage/remarriage, 146–148
Maslow, Abraham, 116
McClellan, W. J., 175

Index

McDonald's, 107
McDonnell Douglas, 51
Medicaid, 156–157
Medicare, 45, 139, 152, 157
Megatrends, 4
Menninger, Karl, 118
mental stress, 110
mergers, 61–62, 131
Merrill Lynch, 42
Mexican wages, 39
Michigan Supreme Court, 110
midlevel management, 51
Miles, Raymond E., 103, 104
Mintz, David, 76
Mitchell, Richard F., 40
Mobil Corporation, 39
money attitudes, 125, 129, 130
Money magazine, 14
monkey research, 175
Montagu, M. F. Ashley, 175
Montgomery Ward and Company, 39
motivational connectors, 120–121

N

Nabisco, 98
Naisbitt, John, 4
National Retail Merchants Association, 40
Natural Death Act, 159
natural resources, 23, 34–35
NBC (National Broadcasting Company), 42, 63
need for touch, 175–176
need to be needed, 174–175
needs, 116, 118, 173–176
New Age economic conditions, 37–56
New Age economic variables, 33–36
New Age Economy, 19–36
New Age financial strategies, 129–131, 133, 161–163
New York Stock Exchange, 41
niche, finding your, 71–73
"niched" markets, 28

Northwestern Mutual Life Career School, 182
N. V. Phillips, 63

O

organizer profile, 167–168
Owens-Illinois, 50
Owens, Jesse, 74

P

Pacific Stock Exchange, 41
packaging yourself for impact, 76–84
Parlophone, 76
participatory management, 177–178
partnerships, business, 70
paternity/maternity leave, 107
Pension Benefit Guaranty Corporation (PBGC), 151
people (as economic variables in New Age), 33
performance-based reward systems, 109
personal articles floater, 143
personal injury protection (PIP), 144
personality, 78–79
personality behavior styles, 166–173
Philip Morris, 61, 98
Phillips Petroleum, 50
Pleitz, Dr. James, 173
positive attitude, 79–80
Poverty of Affluence, The, 165
power of attorney, 128, 140–141, 147, 160
power positioning, 61–66, 114, 164
power, shared, 23, 33
preferred provider organization (PPO), 98, 138, 139
prenuptial agreement, 146, 147–148, 150
Priddy, Robert T., 47
Proactive Systems Incorporated, 99
Probable Life Events (PLEs), 125, 127, 128, 129, 131–161
Proctor and Gamble, 39
product development/failure, 50, 52
production, speed of, 51

productivity, 97, 98
professional connectors, 121–122
"Profile of Older Americans, A," 27
property loss, 141–145
prosperity, targeted, 46–49, 125
public speaking, 83, 88–89
public television, 42

Q
qualified voluntary employee contribution (QVECs), 155

R
rapidity of change, 5–6
rat research, 175
Reagan, Ronald, 122, 123
relater profile, 171–173
relational skills, 82, 164–187
Research Institute of America, 149, 165
resource connectors, 113–123
resumés, 85
retailing industry, 39–40
retirement: 151–155; asset level at, 152–153; early, 38, 49, 50; income assessment, 151–152; phased, 107
ripple effect, 48
Robert Half International, 97
Robins, Philip, 150
robotics, 28, 31, 34, 46, 56, 99–100
role modeling connectors, 115–116

S
sabbaticals, 107
Sakowitz, 39
Salk, Jonas, 30
Saturn concept, 41
Sears, 42, 55, 63
Second Wave economic conditions, 22–23
Second Wave Economy, 9–10, 12, 13, 14, 20
Securities and Exchange Commission, 41, 121, 164, 165–166
security, 124, 125
self-control, 83–84

self-esteem, 79, 116, 132, 180, 183–186
self-esteem connectors, 119
self-fulfillment, 29, 116
self-promotion, 84–90
shelf-life, 49–52, 72
Shell Oil Company, 34
skills clusters, creating market for, 74–76
skills clusters, marketable, 71–74, 102, 103
SME Digest, 52
Smith, Roger, 40
social connectors, 116–117
Social Security Administration, 133, 147, 150, 157
Social Security benefits, 26, 53, 137, 140, 151, 152, 153, 157, 160
social shifts, 20–22, 23–33
Southern California Edison, 34, 98
spiritual connectors, 122–123
SRI International, 99, 128
Stanard and Associates, 102
Stanley, Thomas, 113
steel industry, 44
stock options trading, 41
stress, coping with, 97, 132
subcontracted employee labor, 107–108
substantive workers, 101, 103
Sumitomo Corporation, 63
Sun Exploration and Production Company, 62
Superior Oil Company/Mobil Oil Company, 61
"synergism," 113

T
teaching techniques, 103
team player, 69, 90–94
technological innovation, 24–26, 45, 100, 101, 164
technological interconnectedness, 100, 123
Techtran Corporation, 100

Index

telecommunications, 46, 48, 62
Texas Instruments, 50
Texas Refinery, 105
Texas Supreme Court, 109
textiles industry, 43–44
Think and Grow Rich, 113
Third Wave, The, 7
threshold messaging system, 99
T-I-M-E, 173
time investment, 173–174
time management, 83
Titanic, 126
Toastmasters, 83
Toffler, Alvin, 7, 9
Tofu, Time, Inc., 76
touch, need for, 175–176
tourism, 48
transfer tax, 160
Travelers Insurance Company, 105
Trintex, 63
Truman, Harry, 94
trust in relationships, 186–187
trust officer, 129, 158
TRW Incorporated, 109, 178
21st Century Robotics, 100
Twinkies, 75

U

umbrella policy, 145–146
University of California at Berkeley, 103
University of California at Los Angeles (UCLA), 77
University of Texas at Dallas, 62

Upwardly Mobile Professionals (UMPs), 102
U.S. Bureau of Labor Statistics, 38, 51, 101, 110
U.S. Supreme Court, 110

V

values connectors, shared, 117–118
values synchronization, 176–178
Van O'Steen and Partners, 98
voice-activated office machines, 99
Volcker, Paul, 43
voluntary reduced work time, 106
volunteer activity, 89

W

Wachtel, Paul, 165
Wang Laboratories, 62
Waring Blender, 75
Waring, Fred, 75
Weininger, Otto, 175
White House Conference on Aging (1981), 155
work, changing nature of, 110–111
work force, shifting, 101–110
work options, 106–109
work place, redefinition, 99–101
work sites, remote, 100
writing articles, 87
writing books, 88

X

Xerox Corporation, 107

Z

Zale Corporation, 40